Electric Vehicles Explained

A STRAIGHFORWARD GUIDE TO OWNING AND OPERATING AN ELECTRIC VEHICLE

Welcome to Electric Vehicles Explained.

Whether you're new to EVs or just looking for easy-to-follow tips, this book seeks to empower you to drive with confidence, enjoy the benefits of electric vehicles, and make the most of your car.

This book bridges the gap between traditional cars and electric vehicles.

It explores why we need alternatives to fossil fuels and explains the issues caused by their continued use.

It's designed to offer a simple guide to owning and using electric cars, with enough detail to boost understanding and satisfy your curiosity.

Key terms, points of interest, safety warnings, and tips are provided throughout to help support the information presented.

Owning an EV is a rewarding and empowering step towards modern, sustainable living.

With these simple tips, you'll quickly get the hang of the electric car lifestyle.

Enjoy the journey!

Preface

THIS BOOK OFFERS:

Numerous illustrations and images that enhance understanding and learning.

Clear and simple information for beginners about owning and driving electric cars.

Easy-to-understand explanations to help you learn about electric vehicles.

Lots of pictures and diagrams to make things easier to follow.

Text © Graham Stoakes 2025

Original illustrations © Graham Stoakes 2025

The rights of Graham Stoakes to be identified as author of this work have been asserted by them in accordance with the Copyright, Designs and Patents Act 1988.

Copyright notice ©

All rights reserved. No part of this publication may be reproduced in any form or by any means (including photocopying or storing it in any medium by electronic means and whether or not transiently or incidentally to some other use of this publication) without the written permission of the copyright owner, except in accordance with the provisions of the Copyright, Designs and Patents Act 1988 or under the terms of a license issued by the Copyright Licensing Agency, Saffron House, 6 - 10 Kirby Street, London EC1N 8TS (www.cla.co.uk). Applications for the copyright owners' written permission should be addressed to the author.

Electric Vehicles Explained

Preface

ACKNOWLEDGEMENTS

Graham Stoakes would like to thank the following for their support during this project.

Thank you, George Thurman Co-founder of Women Drive Electric, for the inspiration to write this book. https://womendriveelectric.co.uk/

Thank you, Nathan Ross and Jamie Cushenan of No More Copyright for help with images. https://nomorecopyright.com/

Thank you to alerrandre for the cover design.

Cover image: Shutterstock – Maxger

ABOUT THE AUTHOR

Graham Stoakes AAE MIMI QTLS is a technical trainer/lecturer and author of college textbooks in automotive engineering for light vehicles and motorcycles. With his background as a qualified Master Technician, senior automotive manager, and specialist diagnostic trainer, he brings over 40 years of technical industry experience to this title.

www.grahamstoakes.com

Cover design - fiverr.com/alerrandre

Published by Graham Stoakes

First published 2025

First edition

ISBN 978-0-9929492-8-0

Electric Vehicles Explained

Table of Contents

Preface   1

Introduction and How to Use This Book   5

Quick Start Guide   7

Chapter 1. Why Go Electric? - Uncover the numerous benefits of switching to an electric vehicle, from environmental advantages to long-term cost savings.   **14**

Chapter 2. Choosing the Right EV for You - Navigate the exciting world of electric cars and find the perfect match for your lifestyle and needs.   **36**

Chapter 3. Easy Charging Basics - Learn the ins and outs of charging your EV, including types of chargers, where to find them, and how to ensure you always have enough power.   **57**

Chapter 4. Driving an EV: Tips for Beginners - Gain confidence behind the wheel with practical driving tips tailored specifically for electric vehicles.   **84**

Chapter 5. Navigating Range Anxiety - Say goodbye to range anxiety with strategies and tools to manage your vehicle's range effectively.   **100**

Chapter 6. Maintenance Made Simple - Discover how maintaining an EV is different from traditional cars and enjoy the simplicity and ease of EV upkeep.   **113**

Chapter 7. Building Confidence as an EV Driver - Boost your confidence on the road with advice on building your skills and knowledge as an electric vehicle driver.   **140**

Introduction
How to Use This Book

This book shares the latest information on electric vehicle technology, but remember, technology is always changing. It's designed to help those thinking about or already owning and driving electric or hybrid vehicles. It provides the essential knowledge and skills to help safely use and drive electric cars, but it doesn't replace your vehicle manufacturer's instructions. It's crucial to follow all legal rules for driving and owning cars, including licensing, insurance, road rules, vehicle condition, and safety. Additionally, when charging an electric vehicle, you may need to follow local health and safety rules and bylaws.

Electric vehicles use high-voltage systems that can be dangerous if not handled properly. These systems could cause serious injury or even death if you touch them directly. However, EVs are designed with safety features like warning stickers to help keep you informed about potential dangers. Generally, electric vehicles are safe to drive and use if they are in good condition and have not been tampered with. Never try to repair or access the electric drive system yourself. Only qualified and licensed technicians should perform maintenance or repairs on these parts.

 The information in these sections highlights safety warnings or considerations when operating or driving electric vehicles. The advice aims to minimise the risk of injury or damage to vehicles and equipment. Even if specific safety advice is not provided, evaluate any potential risks before operating or driving an electric car. Always follow the manufacturer's instructions and comply with any legal requirements or regulations.

Electric Vehicles Explained

Introduction
How to Use This Book

The guidance in these sections is intended to support the information about the construction and function of electric vehicle systems. It provides material that enhances understanding and strengthens knowledge of system components and operation.

This feature explains the key terms related to electric vehicle operation, components, and driving. Correctly using technical vocabulary is the foundation for effective understanding. Words highlighted in **bold** within the text are defined here.

These tips offer useful advice for effective driving and operation of electric vehicles.

Although not all of them may be relevant to your current use or vehicle style, they may inspire ideas that you can adapt to your own personal situation, as long as it is safe to do so.

As the driver or owner of an electric car, follow these simple steps to get started and enjoy an efficient, eco-friendly drive.

Quick Start Guide

INITIAL SETUP

Charging the Battery:

Step 1
- Find the charging port on the car (usually at the front or side). It might open with a lever or a switch.

Step 2
- Determine the type of plug or socket you have (check the *types* of chargers available).

Step 3
- Connect the charging cable from your home charger or a public charging station.

Step 4
- Look at the dashboard display to see the charging status and the time needed for a full charge.

When using a DC fast charger, the battery may only charge to 80%.

This is for safety reasons and also prolongs the lifespan of the drive battery.

Key Functions
- Your car might use a regular key fob or a digital key through a phone app. Just keep the key fob or phone with you to unlock and start the car.

Electric Vehicles Explained

Quick Start Guide

🔧 **Adjust Settings:**

Step 1
- Adjust the seats, mirrors, and steering wheel for comfort.

Step 2
- Set up your preferences for heating, ventilation and air conditioning HVAC.

Step 3
- Sync your mobile device via Bluetooth for hands-free calls andentertainment.

Step 4
- Set up your preferences on the infotainment system (navigation, radio,etc.).

DRIVING THE CAR

⏻ **Starting the Car:**

Step 1
- Press the brake pedal and then the start button to power up the car.

Step 2
- The dashboard will light up, indicating the car is ready to drive.

Electric Vehicles Explained

Quick Start Guide

🎮 Select Driving Mode:

Step 1
- With your foot on the brake, use the gear selector to choose "D" (Drive),
- "R" (Reverse), or "P" (Park).

Step 2
- Some cars have additional modes like "Eco," "Sport," or "Normal" fordifferent driving experiences. Make your selection if available.

⏭ Accelerating and Braking:

Step 1
- Once you take your foot off the brake pedal, the car will start moving on its own.

Step 2
- Gently press the accelerator pedal to start moving.

Step 3
- Electric cars often have something called regenerative braking; thismeans that when you lift your foot off the accelerator, the car will slow down and recharge the battery.

Step 4
- Use the brake pedal just like you would in a regular car to stop more smoothly.

Electric Vehicles Explained

Quick Start Guide

 Stay alert to the road and what's around you; since electric cars are so quiet, people might not hear you coming. Always keep an eye on how much energy you have left, and the range shown on your dashboard. Plan your routes in advance, especially for longer trips, and make sure you know where the charging stations are. Use regenerative braking to save energy every chance you get.

CHARGING THE CAR

 Finding Charging Stations:

Step 1
- Use your car's satnav or a charging station app to find nearby chargers.

Step 2
- If using a public charger, make sure you have a way to pay. This might mean downloading an app beforehand.

Step 3
- Plan ahead to avoid running low on battery.

Charging at Home:
- Plug into a standard wall outlet (slow charge) or install a special home charger (faster charge).
- Charging overnight is convenient and ensures your battery is full each day.
- You can top up the battery whenever you want; you don't have to wait for it to be empty.

Electric Vehicles Explained

Quick Start Guide

> **Charging on th Go:**
> - Follow the same process as at home: find the charging port, plug in the cable, and keep an eye on the charging status.
> - Fast chargers can really reduce the time it takes to charge your car, often reaching 80% charge in less than 30 minutes.

MAINTENANCE AND SAFETY

To keep your electric car running smoothly and safely, perform these regular checks:

Check tyre pressure and tread often.

Make sure all lights and indicators are working properly.

Keep an eye on fluid levels, like windscreen washer and brake fluid.

 Software Updates:

- Keep your car's software updated for the best performance and new features.
- Most updates can be done over-the-air or through your service provider.

Following these tips will help ensure your electric vehicle remains in top condition and safe to drive. Remember, regular maintenance and updates are key to a happy, healthy electric car.

 Safety Reminders:

Always wear your seatbelt and make sure all passengers do the same.

Keep your focus on the road and avoid distractions.

Get to know the emergency procedures in your owner's manual.

Electric Vehicles Explained

Quick Start Guide

While electric vehicles are designed with safety in mind, they can have risks that you might not expect with traditional cars. It's important to remember that accidents happen, and ignoring or bypassing safety warnings can be dangerous. Never try to work on or take apart the electric vehicle's drive components or systems meant to keep you safe. Always follow the manufacturer's warnings and don't remove any safety labels.

Dangers include, but are not limited to:

Electrocution – When someone is injured or killed by electric shock.

The drive system of an electric vehicle uses high voltages that can be deadly. Just like the electricity in homes or businesses, the dangerous parts are covered or insulated to keep you safe. EVs are designed with care to ensure these high voltage parts are shielded from daily use. Still, areas like the engine or motor bays might have exposed high voltage wires. These wires are often coated in bright orange to indicate danger, so avoid touching or disturbing them.

Fire – A situation where something catches fire, producing light, heat, and flames.

Vehicle fires can happen with any type of car, but EVs actually catch fire less often than traditional cars. The battery is the biggest fire risk, but fires starting in the battery are rare. Once a battery catches fire, it's harder to put out and produces toxic smoke. Regular fire extinguishers might not work on EV fires. Call the emergency services and leave the situation to trained firefighters.

Chemicals – Substances produced or used in reactions.

EV batteries use chemicals to store electricity, which can be poisonous, toxic, and highly corrosive.

Electric Vehicles Explained

Quick Start Guide

They can cause serious burns or blindness if they come into contact with your skin or eyes. The risk of exposure is very low unless the vehicle is in an accident, or someone tampers with the battery.

Magnetic fields – Areas around a magnet or moving electric charge where magnetic forces act.

Electricity and magnetism are closely linked. Powerful magnets in EV motors and the electric current in circuits create strong electromagnetic fields. These fields can interfere with life-saving devices like pacemakers, defibrillators, and insulin pumps. Generally, these fields are shielded from the driver, making EVs safe to use. People with these devices should avoid working on parts of the EV that produce strong electromagnetic fields.

Moving silently – Operating without making any noise.

One advantage of EVs is their almost silent operation when driving, but this can also be a danger for nearby people or pedestrians who might not hear the vehicle approaching. EVs usually have a noise generator that makes a mild hum when moving to alert pedestrians. Some EVs have a switch to turn off this sound, which increases the risk of accidents. Be aware of this feature and use it responsibly.

Tripping – Stumbling or falling after catching your foot on something.

When charging an EV, the cable can be a trip hazard. Try to charge your vehicle in a dedicated area with clear warnings. If that's not possible, avoid trailing cables across walkways and follow any health and safety requirements and local regulations.

ENJOY YOUR DRIVE

You'll find more detailed information in the rest of this book, and your owner's manual will have all the instructions you need.

Electric Vehicles Explained

Chapter 1. Why Go Electric?

Electric cars actually came before petrol-powered cars, being used in the late 19th and early 20th centuries. However, as the car assembly line became common, petrol/gasoline cars became cheaper and more available, which led to a decline in the use of electric vehicles.

Despite this setback, the seeds of innovation were planted. The need for cleaner, more sustainable transportation began to re-emerge in the late 20th century, paving the way for a revival in electric vehicle technology.

The 21st Century has marked a significant turning point for electric cars. This change is driven by better battery technology, growing worries about climate change, and new laws to protect the environment.

Innovations in battery design have improved how much energy electric cars can store and reduced costs, making them more affordable for everyone.

Charging at home is convenient for many people.

Financial benefits also encourage the use of electric cars. Some programs offer tax breaks and rebates for buying EVs and charging systems, helping with the initial cost. Additionally, electric vehicles usually have lower running costs because they use less fuel and need less maintenance.

Electric Vehicles Explained

Chapter 1.
Why Go Electric?

Many people are starting to see the benefits of electric vehicles. They are not only better for the environment but can also save you money in the long run.

Modern EVs have come a long way, losing the old image of being slow and boring. Today, electric cars are quick, handle well, and look stylish.

Plus, they are much quieter than traditional cars, making for a peaceful drive.

BACKGROUND

To better understand how electric cars work and their benefits, it's helpful to know a bit about electricity and some related terms.

Energy

Electricity is a form of energy that makes things work. We use it in our daily lives to power everything from household gadgets to cars. It's a clean and efficient source of energy.

What is electricity?

Electricity is the flow of small particles called electrons through a material, like a wire. To understand how electricity works, we need to know a few key ideas: **voltage**, **current**, **resistance** and **power**.

Simply put, electricity is a basic energy source found in **atoms** and is closely related to magnetism.

Electric Vehicles Explained

Chapter 1.
Why Go Electric?

Voltage is like the pressure that pushes electricity through a wire, helping it to flow and do work.

Current is the flow of electricity, or electrons, through a material, like water flowing through a pipe.

Resistance is like a roadblock that slows down the flow of electricity through a wire, similar to how obstacles slow down traffic on a road.

Power is the rate at which energy is used or produced. It shows how quickly electricity can work to do things like lighting up a bulb or running a machine.

Atoms are the tiny building blocks that make up everything around us. They are like tiny Legos that join to form different materials and objects.

The Discovery of electricity

About 2500 years ago, a Greek scientist named Thales discovered that rubbing amber (fossilised tree sap) with a cloth attracted small dust and fluff particles. This was his discovery of static electricity. While Thales did not fully understand the phenomenon, he did document his findings.

Chapter 1.
Why Go Electric?

Around 1550, William Gilbert, who was Queen Elizabeth I's doctor, discovered that rubbing a silk cloth on a glass rod could attract even heavier objects, like feathers. He called this phenomenon 'electricus', taking the name from the Greek word for amber, 'elektron', and leading to the word electricity.

While static electricity is interesting, it's hard to convert into a usable energy source because electricity needs to move to be useful.

In the late 18th century, two Italian scientists, Luigi Galvani and Alessandro Volta, were competing and ended up creating the first moving electricity, known as electric current. This electric current was produced through a chemical reaction and eventually led to the invention of the battery.

Electricity might sound complicated because it exists in tiny atoms, but let's break it down.

Imagine an atom like a miniature solar system: the **nucleus** is the sun, and the **electrons** are planets orbiting around it. The nucleus has positively charged **protons** and neutral **neutrons**, while the electrons are negatively charged. When these electrons move from one atom to another, they create an electric current.

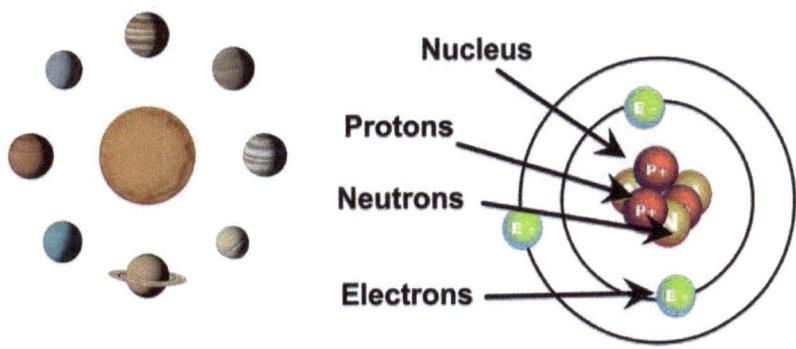

Electric Vehicles Explained

Chapter 1.
Why Go Electric?

The **nucleus** is the centre of an atom, like the sun in a solar system. It contains protons and neutrons, which are tiny particles.

Electrons are tiny particles that orbit around the centre of an atom, and they carry a negative electrical charge.

Protons are tiny particles found in the centre of an atom that carry a positive electrical charge.

Neutrons are tiny particles found in the nucleus of an atom that have no electrical charge, making them neutral.

ATOMS AND MOLECULES

Every substance is made up of **molecules**, which in turn are composed of atoms. For example, water is a molecule named H2O, consisting of two hydrogen (H) atoms and one oxygen (O) atom.

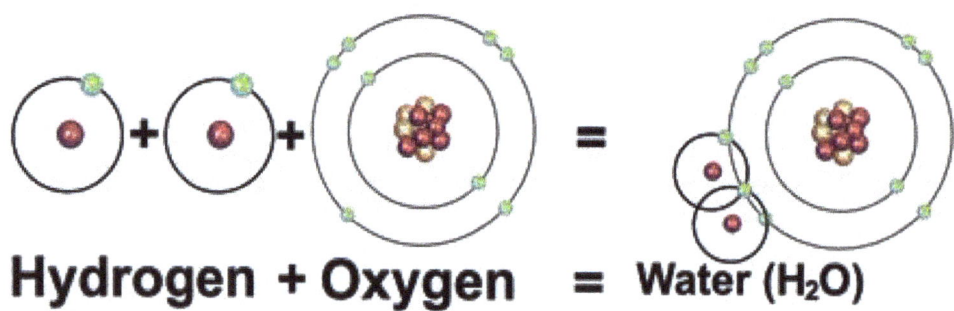

Hydrogen + Oxygen = Water (H_2O)

Electric Vehicles Explained

Chapter 1.
Why Go Electric?

Movement of electrons

To generate an electric current, electrons need to move from one atom to another. Electron movement requires an external force or pressure, which can be created by **magnetic fields** or a chemical reaction.

Electrons orbit the nucleus of an atom, like how planets orbit the sun due to gravity. In some atoms with simple structures, the attraction between the nucleus and electrons is very strong, making it difficult for electrons to move.

Elements where electrons don't move easily are known as **insulators**.

Other atoms, however, have a weaker attraction force between the nucleus and electrons within their structure. When electrons move easily between atoms, the element is known as a **conductor**.

For electrons to move from one atom to another, they need a continuous unbroken loop or path, known as a **circuit**. This allows an electron to be replaced by another one from behind as it moves when switched on. Without a complete circuit, electrons can't flow because the last electron in the conductor has nowhere to go. If the circuit is interrupted, the current stops and the electricity is effectively switched off.

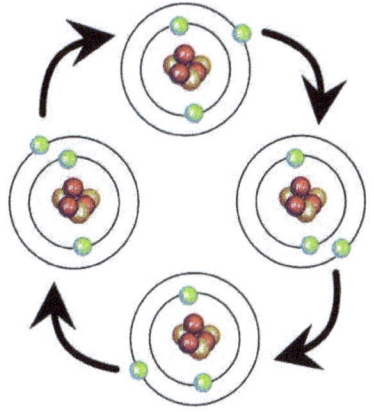

Electric Vehicles Explained

Chapter 1.
Why Go Electric?

Electricity and magnetism are closely related, like two sides of the same coin. Magnetism is an invisible force that can attract or repel certain metals. Both electricity and magnetism have positive and negative poles, or north and south, and both are able to pull together or push apart.

When a magnet passes a copper conductor (wire), the magnetic attraction moves electrons through the conductor, creating an electric current. On the other hand, when an electric current passes through a copper conductor, it generates an invisible magnetic field. The magnetic effect of an electric current can cause movement through attraction or repulsion. This movement can be harnessed to create a **motor**.

Similarly, the movement of magnets past a conductor can generate an electric current, which is the principle behind a **generator**.

- Motors convert electrical energy into mechanical energy.
- Generators convert mechanical energy into electrical energy.

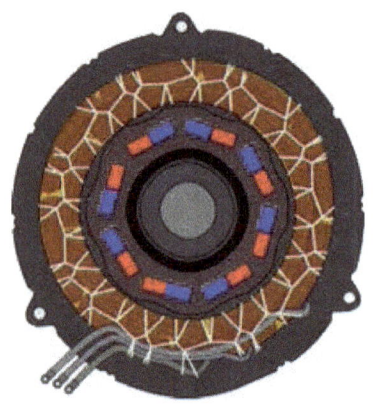

Electric Vehicles Explained

Chapter 1.
Why Go Electric?

Molecules are tiny particles made up of two or more atoms bonded together. They form every substance around us, including water, air, and living organisms.

Magnetic fields are invisible forces that can pull or push certain metals without actually touching them. They are created by magnets or when electricity flows through a wire.

Insulators are materials that do not allow electricity to flow through them easily because the electrons are tightly bound to their atoms.

Conductors are materials that allow electricity to flow through them easily because their electrons can move freely between atoms.

A **circuit** is a closed loop that allows electricity to flow continuously without interruption.

A **motor** is a device that converts electrical energy into movement or mechanical energy, making machines and EVs work.

A **generator** is a machine that turns movement into electricity, allowing us to power devices when plugged in. It works by spinning magnets near wires to create the electric current.

Chapter 1.
Why Go Electric?

CHEMICAL REACTIONS

You can also store electrical energy in a battery, which acts like a chemical container for energy. This stored energy can be carried around and used whenever you need it. The best part is this process works both ways: you can put energy into the battery and take it out again to power your devices and car.

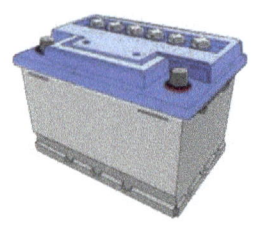

IMPORTANT TERMS

With the operation and use of electric vehicles, it's important to understand some common electrical terms. These terms often relate to the units of measurement used when describing electrical functions and are sometimes compared to water flowing in pipes to help make sense of them – water being the electricity, and a pipe being the wire.

Volts

Volts, named after Italian scientist Alessandro Volta, refers to the pressure pushing electricity through a circuit. Think of it like water pressure pushing its way through a pipe.

Amps

Amps, named after French physicist André-Marie Ampère, refers to the amount of electricity flowing in a circuit. Imagine it as the amount of water flowing through a pipe.

Electric Vehicles Explained

Chapter 1.
Why Go Electric?

Ohms

Ohms, named after German physicist Georg Ohm, is about the restriction of electric current, called resistance. Think of squeezing a hosepipe while water is flowing through it. Resistance is generally not desirable as it reduces the electricity available to do useful work.

Watts

Watts, named after Scottish engineer James Watt, measures power produced or used. Power is about how hard something is working. James Watt improved steam engines and compared their effort to that of a horse, leading to the term 'horsepower'.

Charge

Charge refers to the amount of electricity passing through a conductor in one second. It's officially measured in coulombs, named after French engineer Charles-Augustin de Coulomb, but this term is rarely mentioned when talking about electric vehicles. The word charge is often used to describe filling up a car's battery or the speed of charging and discharging.

Electric Vehicles Explained

Chapter 1.
Why Go Electric?

Here's a simple way to remember the basics of electricity:

- Volts are like the pressure pushing electricity through a wire.

- Amps are the amount of electricity flowing through the wire.

- Ohms measure how much the wire resists that flow.

- Watts show how much power is being used or produced.

Just think of it like water in a hosepipe: volts are the water pressure, amps are the amount of water flowing, ohms are the pinch in the hose that slows the water down, and watts are the power of the water spraying out.

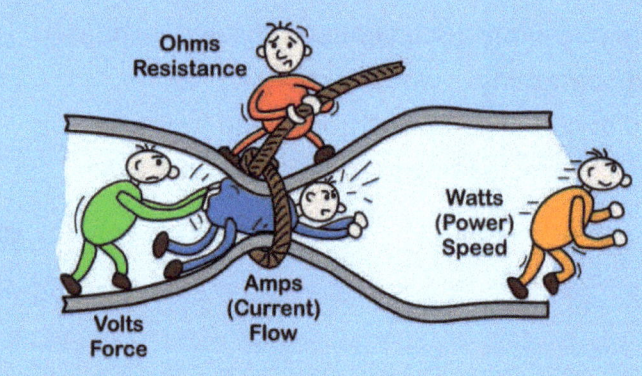

Kilowatt hours KWh

How much electricity is used when driving an electric car is often calculated in kilowatt hours, or KWh. This tells you how much energy the car uses over time and distance. Traditional cars use miles per gallon (MPG) or kilometres per litre (KM/L) to show fuel efficiency, while electric cars use miles or kilometres per kilowatt hour. However, these values are not directly comparable. (See KWh verses MPG)

Electric Vehicles Explained

Chapter 1.
Why Go Electric?

AC AND DC

Electric current is the flow of electricity and can be thought of like water flowing through a pipe. It comes in two forms: alternating current (AC) and direct current (DC). This flow of electricity is what makes electrical devices work.

What is the difference and where will you find it?

Alternating current (AC) is when electricity flows back and forth, while direct current (DC) flows in one direction only.

Most electrical devices don't mind which way the current flows as long as there's power. However, devices made for AC use AC, and those made for DC use DC.

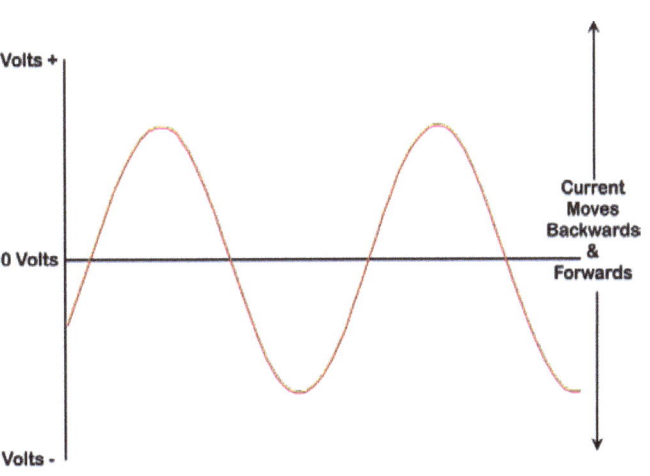

AC is created using generators and is found in the electricity that powers your home.

It can't be stored and is made as needed, meaning power stations must keep an eye on demand and adjust their output.

Because AC can't be stored, it's not used in batteries for electric cars.

Electric Vehicles Explained

Chapter 1.
Why Go Electric?

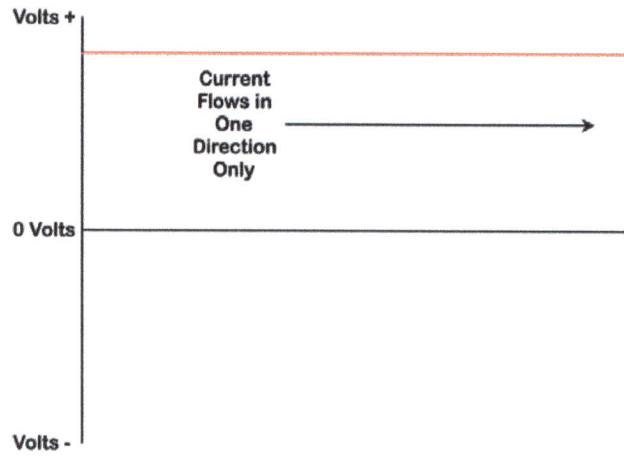

DC, on the other hand, is produced by chemical reactions in batteries. This makes it perfect for electric cars, but it means the batteries need to be **recharged** regularly.

When you charge an electric car, the AC from your home needs to be changed to DC to store in the battery. This is called **rectification**.

Electric cars often use AC motors because they work better for different driving conditions. This means the DC from the battery has to be changed back to AC to run the motor. This change is called **inversion**.

The device that changes DC to AC and AC to DC in electric cars is called an inverter.

Recharged means to fill a battery with electrical energy so it can be used again.

Rectification is the process of changing alternating current (AC) into direct current (DC).

Inversion is the process of changing direct current (DC) back to alternating current (AC) in electric cars to run the motor.

Electric Vehicles Explained

Chapter 1.
Why Go Electric?

POLLUTION AND THE ENVIRONMENT

It is widely believed that human activity significantly affects the Earth's climate. Pollution from vehicles plays a big role in this. While no vehicle is completely emission-free, electric vehicles have been shown to have a much lower impact on the environment throughout their entire lifecycle, from production to disposal, compared to traditional petrol/gasoline or diesel cars.

Climate change

Climate change is the term used to describe long-term changes in the planet's weather patterns and temperatures. While some of these changes can happen naturally, it's been proven that human activities and pollution, especially since the industrial revolution, are the main cause. Climate change not only impacts the environment but also leads to more frequent extreme weather events, which often result in natural disasters.

Electric Vehicles Explained

Chapter 1.
Why Go Electric?

Global warming

This is an environmental phenomenon which causes the Earth's temperature to rise.

Global warming is often confused with weather, leading some people to argue that cold winters disprove its existence. However, measurements show that worldwide average temperatures are increasing every year. While scientists agree it is happening, they have different views on how much temperatures will rise. Predictions for the next century suggest an increase of between 2°C and 10°C, and an increase of about 6°C could lead to a global extinction!

The main cause of global warming is the greenhouse effect.

The greenhouse effect

This is a natural process that warms the Earth's surface.

It happens because the Earth gets most of its energy from the sun's rays, which area type of radiation. Radiation is energy that travels in waves. The distance between these waves decides what kind of energy it is.

Higher frequency waves (waves that are close together) can pass through things easily. For example, X-rays can go through soft tissue but are blocked by bones, letting us see images of our skeleton.

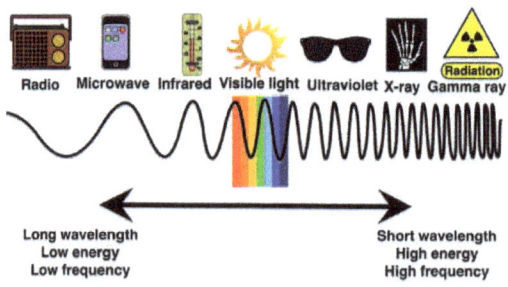

Electric Vehicles Explained

Chapter 1.
Why Go Electric?

The sun's rays, mainly in the form of visible light, travel easily through the Earth's atmosphere and heat the ground. At night, this heat is sent back into space as **infrared radiation**, which has a longer wavelength than visible light. Certain gases in our atmosphere trap this infrared radiation, causing the Earth to warm up, and this is called the greenhouse effect.

The main gases that cause the greenhouse effect are:

- Methane

- Water vapour

- Carbon dioxide (CO_2)

You can see the greenhouse effect in action on cloudy nights when it's warmer because water vapour traps the heat, unlike on clear nights when most of the heat escapes.

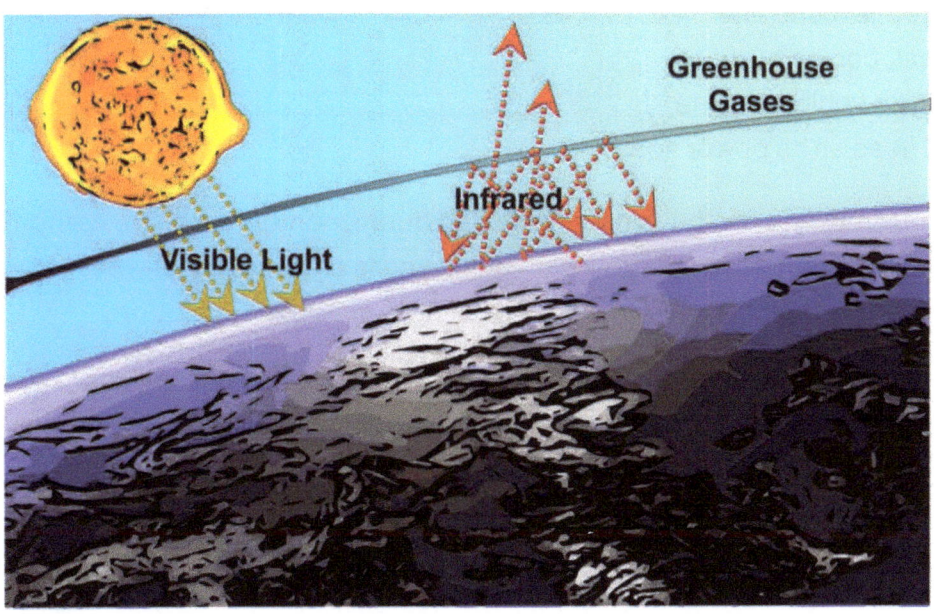

Chapter 1.
Why Go Electric?

FOSSIL FUELS

This is the name given to fuels made from crude oil extracted from underground. This oil has formed over millions of years from biological (once-living organisms), both plant and animal life which have decomposed under high pressure and heat.

Crude oil provides a rich source of **hydrocarbon** molecules which, once processed into petrol/gasoline and diesel, can be burned inside a vehicle engine and used as its power source.

Unfortunately, only the hydrogen is used during combustion. The carbon can be thought of as the fuels packaging and is disposed of as waste mainly from exhaust emissions, which leads to environmental **pollution**.

Traditional vehicles which use an internal combustion engine (ICE) operating with petrol/gasoline or diesel, produce exhaust emissions which can be harmful to both humans and the environment.

Chapter 1.
Why Go Electric?

Infrared radiation is a type of energy that we feel as heat, and it is invisible to the human eye. It is emitted by all objects, with warmer objects emitting more infrared radiation than cooler ones.

A **hydrocarbon** is a chemical compound made up of hydrogen and carbon atoms. It is the main component of fuels like petrol/gasoline and diesel.

Pollution is the harmful introduction of contaminants into the environment, which can damage natural resources, harm wildlife, and affect human health.

EXHAUST GASSES

Toxic and environmentally polluting chemicals produced by internal combustion engines (ICE) include – HC CO NOx SO2 (and CO2).

Hydrocarbons (HC)

Both petrol/gasoline and diesel are made of hydrocarbons. When these fuels are burned in vehicle engines, the process isn't perfect. Small amounts of hydrocarbons escape through the exhaust and into the air. Breathing in these chemicals can make it hard to breathe and lower your blood oxygen levels. This can cause confusion or even seizures, and long-term exposure to hydrocarbons can lead to cancer.

Sulphur dioxide (SO2)

This pollutant can sometimes be produced when burning fossil fuels. Sulphur dioxide can be harmful to humans if inhaled in large amounts. It also contributes to acid rain and can worsen climate change.

Chapter 1.
Why Go Electric?

Carbon monoxide (CO)

Carbon monoxide is a harmful gas produced when a car engine doesn't burn fuel completely. This gas is colourless and odourless, so it can be hard to detect. Breathing in carbon monoxide can cause symptoms like headaches, dizziness, confusion, or chest pain. In large amounts, it can lead to unconsciousness, seizures, or even death.

Oxides of nitrogen (Nox)

This refers to gases created when oxygen and nitrogen combine because of the high heat in car engines. These gases can harm both people and the environment. They can make it hard to breathe, cause inflammation, and can even affect your heart. In the environment, these gases can lead to acid rain, which harms nature.

Carbon dioxide (CO2)

While not necessarily toxic, carbon dioxide (CO2) from human activities is a major cause of global warming. In small amounts, it has minimal effect, but the large quantities produced by vehicles significantly contribute to climate change. This issue arises from burning fossil fuels in engines. Ironically, the more efficient an engine is, the more CO2 it tends to produce.

ALTERNATIVE FUELS

Alternative fuels are other types of fuel besides traditional petrol/gasoline and diesel. They can come from natural sources or be made in laboratories. Often, they are less polluting than petrol/gasoline or diesel, depending on how they are produced.

Chapter 1.
Why Go Electric?

Examples of alternative fuels include:

- Biodiesel
- Biogas
- Liquified petroleum gas (LPG)
- Compressed natural gas (CNG)
- Alcohol-based fuels
- Synthetic petrol

Electric vehicles (EVs) are often surrounded by myths, one of which is that they merely shift emissions from the roads to power stations. While it is true that the electricity used to charge EVs can come from power plants that emit pollutants, it's important to understand that EVs are still significantly cleaner than traditional petrol/gasoline or diesel vehicles.

The electricity grid is becoming cleaner every year as more renewable energy sources are added. This means that the environmental impact of charging EVs is continuously decreasing. Also, the centralised nature of power stations allows for easier implementation of advanced technologies to capture and reduce emissions compared to millions of individual car engines.

Electric Vehicles Explained

Chapter 1.
Why Go Electric?

PARTICULATE EMISSIONS

These tiny particles come from vehicles when they are used. Breathing them in can harm your health. While particulates come from the exhaust of petrol/gasoline or diesel vehicles, they also come from brakes and tyres on all cars, including electric ones.

This means that no vehicle is completely free from environmental impact, but electric cars do not produce exhaust emissions, which helps reduce the overall amount significantly.

Electric cars use of regenerative braking reduces wear on the vehicles braking components, and therefore the amount of particulate emissions they produce.

Although no vehicle is perfect, switching to partially or fully electric cars can greatly lower the impact on our environment.

Electric Vehicles Explained

Chapter 1.
Why Go Electric?

Many people worry that there aren't enough important minerals, like lithium, cobalt, and nickel, to make all the batteries we need for electric vehicles. But this isn't really something to worry about.

Here's why:

First, as more people buy EVs, companies are doing more mining and finding better ways to get these minerals. There is more investment in mining and processing these minerals in a more efficient and environmentally friendly way.

Second, we are getting better at recycling old batteries. We can take them apart and reuse the valuable materials to make new batteries, which means we won't always need to mine more minerals. This helps create a more sustainable cycle.

Lastly, scientists are working hard to create new kinds of batteries that don't need as many rare minerals or use different materials altogether. Innovations, like solid-state batteries and ones using common elements like sodium, look very promising. So, although making EV batteries requires certain minerals, the combination of improved mining, recycling, and new battery research means we'll have enough to support the growing number of electric vehicles.

CONCLUSION

In summary, switching to alternative fuels and electric cars is vital for reducing the harm caused by traditional fuels. While no car is completely without impact on the environment, using cleaner technology helps us move towards a greener future. By choosing these options, we can make the world healthier and improve our lives.

Electric Vehicles Explained

Chapter 2. Choosing the Right EV for You

WHAT IS AN EV?

Electric vehicles, or EVs, are any kind of transport that runs on electricity, either fully or partly.

This can include everything from basic scooters and bicycles to cars, trucks, ships, and even airplanes.

In the context of road transport, EVs generally refer to cars, vans, trucks, and buses.

These can be hybrids, fully electric vehicles, or those powered by hydrogen fuel cells.

Electric Vehicles Explained

Chapter 2. Choosing the Right EV for You

Hybrid

A hybrid vehicle uses both an engine (petrol/gasoline or diesel) and an electric motor to help it run.

There are three main styles of hybrid vehicle:

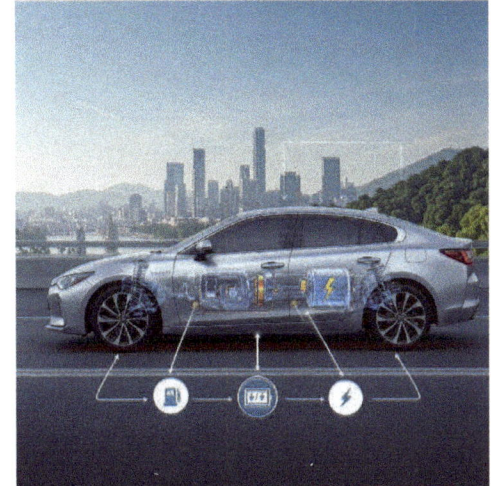

Style one - This basic type of hybrid helps the engine when starting from a stop. It can also capture small amounts of energy when slowing down to recharge the battery. Often called a mild-hybrid, it doesn't offer electric-only driving, so it still uses fuel and produces exhaust emissions like a traditional vehicle.

Style two - Here, the engine mainly drives the vehicle, but the electric motor helps out and reduces the engine's workload. The engine usually switches off when the car is stationary and restarts when needed. This type of hybrid works a lot like a traditional car but is more efficient, reducing exhaust emissions and improving fuel economy. Most of these can drive for short distances using electric power alone.

Style three - This type of hybrid is mostly powered by electricity, but it has an onboard engine that acts like a generator, making electricity when needed. It operates more like a fully electric vehicle but can generate its own electricity, so it doesn't always need to be plugged in to recharge. Since the engine isn't directly driving the car, it produces fewer emissions and uses less fuel. However, the engine's noise might not match the car's speed, which can feel strange at first. This type is often called an extended range electric vehicle or series-hybrid.

Chapter 2. Choosing the Right EV for You

A hybrid is refuelled and driven much like a traditional vehicle, but it also needs an onboard high-voltage battery to support its electric driving.

This battery needs to be recharged as it loses power.

Some hybrids can be plugged into the mains electricity to recharge, but most generate their own electricity while you drive, often called 'self-charging', which can be a bit misleading.

'Self-charging' might make it sound like the car creates electricity by itself with no impact on fuel or the environment, but that's not exactly true.

Most of the electricity needed to recharge the hybrid's battery is made by using its engine, meaning it still burns fuel (petrol/gasoline or diesel).

While this is more economical than a traditional car, it's not as efficient as electricity from a power station. So, plugging in to mains electricity is often a better option.

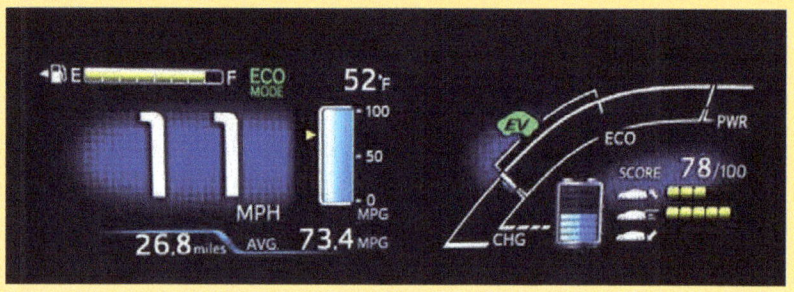

Chapter 2. Choosing the Right EV for You

Compromise

In simple terms, a hybrid car is a middle ground between a traditional petrol/gasoline or diesel car and an electric car. It's a great option for those who might find a fully electric vehicle unsuitable or impractical. Hybrids can be a fantastic first step into the world of electric vehicles, offering a blend of both worlds and making it easier for people to start experiencing the benefits of electric driving.

BATTERY ELECTRIC VEHICLE (BEV)

A battery electric vehicle, or pure EV, gets all of its power from its own battery. Unlike a hybrid, it doesn't have a petrol/gasoline or diesel engine to help drive or charge its battery. This means it needs to be regularly plugged into the electricity grid to keep the battery charged.

The battery powers electric motors that move the car. Since there is no engine, a fully electric vehicle doesn't produce exhaust emissions, making it a zero-emission vehicle (ZEV) when in use. However, it's important to note that the source of the electricity will always have some environmental impact.

Electric Vehicles Explained

Chapter 2. Choosing the Right EV for You

Electricity from renewable sources like solar, wind, or hydroelectric power are the cleanest, but even electricity from a conventional power station is more efficient and cleaner than burning fuel in a traditional engine.

HYDROGEN FUEL CELL (HFC)

A hydrogen fuel cell (HFC) vehicle is basically an electric car that uses hydrogen gas as its power source. Instead of charging the car's battery with mains electricity, you fill up a tank with hydrogen, similar to putting fuel in a traditional car. The car uses a special device called a fuel cell, which mixes hydrogen with oxygen from the air to create water (H_2O). This chemical reaction produces electricity to power the car's electric motors.

Chapter 2. Choosing the Right EV for You

REGENERATIVE BRAKING

Regenerative braking uses the energy that is usually wasted as heat when a car slows down.

In a regular car, brakes turn movement into heat through friction, which slows the vehicle down. This heat is then released into the air, wasting the energy. But if this movement is turned into electricity instead of heat, it can be directed back to the battery, saving energy.

While this is a smart way to use normally wasted energy, it doesn't generate enough to keep the battery fully charged and only provides a small amount of the needed electricity.

OWNING AN EV

Choosing the type of electric car depends on personal needs and preferences. For many, switching from a conventional car to a fully electric vehicle might not be practical straightaway. Luckily, you have many options, including micro/mild hybrids, full hybrids, plug-in hybrids, and hydrogen fuel cell cars, which may not need to be plugged in.

Electric Vehicles Explained

Chapter 2. Choosing the Right EV for You

Here are some things to think about:

Access to charging - Fully electric and plug-in hybrids need regular charging, which can be done at public charge points. However, home charging is often cheaper and more convenient. You can use a slow-speed cable plugged into a normal outlet if you have an access point near the car or a dedicated home charger installed by a professional.

Parking - While some on-road locations have charging options, off-road parking is usually more practical. Charging cables should not cross public walkways to avoid hazards. A private parking space, driveway, or garage makes it easier to charge your vehicle.

Energy tariff - Many energy suppliers offer special rates for charging electric cars, especially during off-peak hours. This can lower the cost of charging. Set timers on your charger or vehicle to use off-peak electricity, and if possible, consider solar power for a green and cost-effective option.

Daily mileage and range - Think about how far you drive each day. Most people use only a small part of the available range daily. If you can charge overnight, you start each day with a full battery. For longer trips, plan charging stops to avoid running low on power.

New or second-hand - Whether to buy new or second-hand depends on your personal situation. Owning the car outright means no monthly payments, but you will need to cover maintenance and breakdown costs. Leasing can get you an up-to-date car with maintenance included, but you might not own it at the end of your contract and could have mileage limits.

Unexpected costs - A fully electric car may have costly battery replacements, but this is usually due to reduced range over time, not outright failure. A battery with 70% capacity still works well for those with low daily range needs.

Chapter 2. Choosing the Right EV for You

Features, style and size - This is personal preference. Electric and hybrid cars often have more tech features than conventional cars, but touchscreens can be distracting while driving. Set up features before you drive to avoid distractions, and practice using shortcuts and voice commands.

In summary, if you find it tough to switch directly to a fully electric vehicle, hybrids offer a great introduction to electric driving. The next section will help you understand how different types of hybrid vehicles work.

WHAT IS A HYBRID?

A hybrid vehicle uses two power sources: a traditional petrol/gasoline or diesel engine and an electric motor. The way these power sources work together varies. Sometimes the electric motor helps the engine run better, and other times the engine generates power for the electric motor. This combination makes hybrids efficient and versatile.

Micro hybrids

A micro hybrid car uses a small electric motor to help the engine. This type of hybrid doesn't work as hard as other hybrids, with the electric motor only providing a little assistance when the car starts or accelerates. The engine will switch off when the car stops and turn back on when you start moving again. This helps save fuel and reduce emissions. Micro hybrids are pretty simple, and they operate on a low voltage of around 14 volts.

Electric Vehicles Explained

Chapter 2. Choosing the Right EV for You

Mild hybrids

A mild hybrid generally has a somewhat stronger motor than micro hybrids.  This type of hybrid helps the engine a bit and recaptures some energy when braking, but it can't run on electric power alone. Mild hybrids use a medium to high voltage, ranging from 48 to 100 volts DC.

Full hybrids

A full hybrid typically has a stronger electric motor. It can help the engine a lot and even run the car by itself for short distances. This means you can drive without using petrol/gasoline for a while. Full hybrids also save energy when you brake, which recharges the battery. They usually work with a voltage higher than 200 volts DC.

Plug-in hybrids

A plug-in hybrid has a powerful motor like full hybrids. These cars can give you a boost and support the engine with regenerative braking. You can also drive them using just the electric motor for longer distances because they have a bigger battery. You can charge them from a regular electrical outlet. Usually, plug-in hybrids work with more than 200 volts DC.

Electric Vehicles Explained

Chapter 2. Choosing the Right EV for You

DIFFERENT TYPES OF HYBRID MODE

When driving a hybrid vehicle, several different terms are used to describe how it works:

Engine stop - this happens when the engine turns off while the car is not moving.

Parallel mode - this is when the electric motor helps the engine run.

Series mode - this is when the engine makes electricity to power the electric motor.

Charge mode - this is when the engine is mainly used to run a generator and charge the high-voltage battery.

Regenerative braking - this is when the electric motor helps slow down the car and uses the energy created to recharge the battery a bit.

These terms help you understand how hybrids save fuel and reduce emissions.

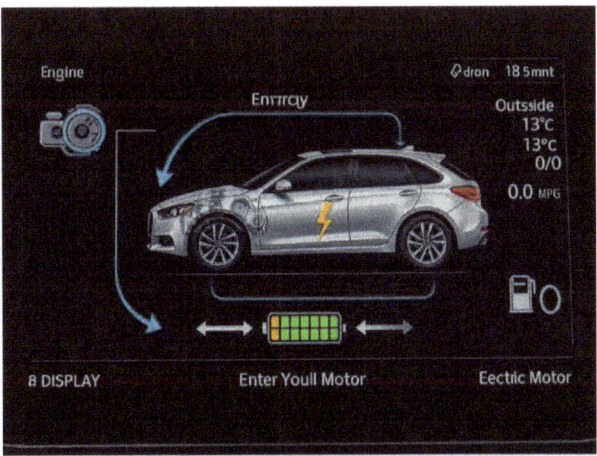

Electric Vehicles Explained

Chapter 2. Choosing the Right EV for You

HYDROGEN AND FUEL CELLS

Hydrogen is a clean and green energy source and can be used like a battery. However, hydrogen in its natural state (H2) would float away into the atmosphere if not contained. Here's how we make and use hydrogen:

1. Separation: Hydrogen is taken out of other compounds using electricity or chemical reactions.

2. Storage: Once separated, it can be stored in containers and used as a portable energy source.

Because it takes energy to separate hydrogen from its source, it's not a fuel on its own.

When hydrogen is used for power, it combines with oxygen from the air, and the only byproduct is water. This means no harmful carbon is released into the air. However, making hydrogen and its source might still release carbon during the process.

Electric Vehicles Explained

Chapter 2. Choosing the Right EV for You

While hydrogen is naturally colourless, colour codes are used to describe how it is made. Here are the codes:

H2 BLACK OR BROWN

This comes from black coal or brown coal, which is very bad for the environment. The process involves heating the coal to break it down, creating gas called **syngas** and carbon dioxide (CO_2).

H2 GREY

Grey hydrogen is made from natural gas, mainly methane (CH_4). This process creates hydrogen (H_2) and carbon dioxide (CO_2) through a method called steam reformation. The CO_2 produced is released into the atmosphere, which is harmful.

H2 BLUE

Blue hydrogen is made like grey hydrogen, but the CO_2 created is captured and stored, rather than released into the air.

H2 GREEN

Green hydrogen is made using clean, renewable energy such as wind, solar, or hydroelectricity. This process, called **electrolysis**, extracts hydrogen from a source material. If only solar power is used, it's sometimes called 'yellow' hydrogen. This method is the best for the environment.

H2 PINK

Pink hydrogen is also made using electrolysis, but the electricity comes from nuclear power, which doesn't emit CO_2 into the air, making it cleaner than grey or blue hydrogen.

Electric Vehicles Explained

Chapter 2. Choosing the Right EV for You

Syngas is a man-made gas mixture mainly composed of hydrogen and carbon dioxide, often used as a fuel source.

Steam reformation is a process where steam is used to break down natural gas into hydrogen and carbon dioxide. It's a common way to produce hydrogen gas.

Electrolysis is a process that uses electricity to split a substance into its basic parts. For example, it can separate water into hydrogen and oxygen.

Storing and transporting hydrogen can be tricky.

It needs to be kept under high pressure or at very low temperatures because, as a gas, hydrogen takes up a lot of space. We use special containers to stop it from leaking over time.

Hydrogen fuel cell (HFC)

A Hydrogen Fuel Cell (HFC) vehicle is a kind of electric car. It works like an electric car but uses a different power source. Instead of a big, heavy battery, it uses hydrogen and oxygen to make electricity.

Chapter 2. Choosing the Right EV for You

In an HFC vehicle, a fuel cell mixes hydrogen from a tank with oxygen from the air.

This reaction, helped by a **catalyst** called a **PEM** or **proton exchange membrane**, produces water, heat, and an electric current.

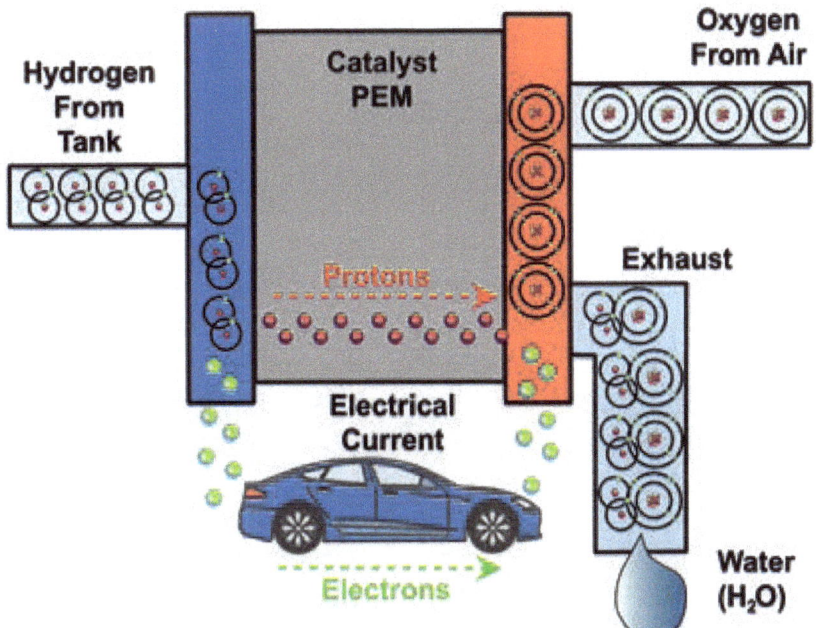

The electricity can either charge a small battery that powers the car or go straight to the motor.

Electric Vehicles Explained

Chapter 2. Choosing the Right EV for You

One big advantage of HFC cars is how they refuel. Unlike regular electric cars that need to be charged, HFC vehicles are refuelled like conventional cars. When the hydrogen runs out, you just refill at a pump, and you're good to go.

A **catalyst** is a substance that helps speed up a chemical reaction without being changed itself. It's like a helper that makes a process happen faster and more efficiently.

A **proton exchange membrane PEM** is a special material used in hydrogen fuel cells. It helps produce electricity by allowing only certain particles (protons) to pass through it while keeping others out. This helps create a reaction that generates power for the car.

Electric Vehicles Explained

Chapter 2. Choosing the Right EV for You

Hydrogen fuel cells (HFCs) are a great alternative to traditional electric cars, but it's a bit of a myth to think they will completely replace them.

Here's why:

Infrastructure - While it's quick to refuel HFC cars, there aren't many hydrogen stations around. Setting up these stations needs a lot of money and time. On the other hand, the charging points for electric cars are already widespread and keep increasing.

Production and efficiency - Making hydrogen takes a lot of energy. The most common way, steam reformation, uses natural gas, which isn't fully clean. Electric cars can use renewable energy like wind or solar power directly, making them more efficient.

Vehicle availability - There are fewer hydrogen fuel cell cars available compared to many electric vehicle models. This means buyers have more choices with electric cars, from budget-friendly to high-end options.

Cost - Producing and storing hydrogen safely is expensive. Meanwhile, batteries for electric cars are getting cheaper, making them more affordable for most people.

Environmental impact - While HFCs only emit water vapour, the overall environmental benefits depend on how the hydrogen is made. If it's made from fossil fuels, it's less green. Electric cars using renewable energy are better for reducing greenhouse gases.

In short, while hydrogen fuel cells are exciting, they won't replace electric cars anytime soon. Both technologies can coexist, providing different benefits and catering to various needs and preferences.

Electric Vehicles Explained

Chapter 2. Choosing the Right EV for You

TEST DRIVE – HINTS AND TIPS – WHAT TO ASK

Choosing an electric car is a big decision, so it's important to make sure it fits your needs. Buying any vehicle is a significant investment, and good research and preparation will help you get the best out of it.

Before test driving

Research models - Look up different electric cars that catch your eye and seem to suit your needs. Ask friends or family who already have an electric car for their opinions. If you're buying new, find some local dealers to visit, or check out second-hand adverts.

Know your budget - Figure out how much you want to spend. Decide if you will lease, finance, or buy the car outright. Think about whether you'll need any extra warranties or maintenance packages.

Charging options - Make sure you have easy access to charging points at home, work, or nearby public spots. Look into the costs and apps for public charging. Hybrid cars might offer more flexibility depending on your situation.

Electric Vehicles Explained

Chapter 2. Choosing the Right EV for You

Understand incentives - Check for any government incentives, rebates, or tax credits for electric cars in your area. This can include support for installing a home charger.

Range needs - Think about your daily commute and how often you drive to pick a car with enough range. With home charging, you can often start each day with a full battery.

Book a test drive - Arrange a test drive with a dealership that has the models you're interested in. Bring a friend for support or a second opinion. Their feedback can be helpful, and it's always good to have someone with you.

During the test drive

Driving experience - Notice the acceleration, handling, and overall driving feel. Remember that an electric car may feel quite different from a traditional car, so give yourself some time to adjust. Ask the seller for any driving tips to help you get the most out of your test drive.

Comfort and space - Check how comfortable the seats are, how much legroom you have, and the space for cargo. Make sure it meets your current needs and think about any future changes in your situation.

Technology and features - Look at the infotainment system, navigation, and advanced features like driver assistance. They should make owning the car easier, not more complicated.

Charging time - Find out how long it takes to charge the car at home (using both slower and faster chargers) and at public fast-charging stations. Charging times can vary depending on the type of charger and the car's ability to handle different speeds.

Chapter 2. Choosing the Right EV for You

Battery life and warranty - Ask about the battery's warranty and how long it is expected to last. Some cars allow you to lease the battery, which can be a good option if you're worried about replacement costs. If you're buying a used car, check if extended warranties are available for the battery.

Questions to ask the dealer

What is the actual range of this car? (It's usually less than what is advertised)

What kind of maintenance does this car need?

How long does it take to charge the battery completely? (Ask about all three charging speeds)

What is the maximum charge speed?

Does the car get software updates? How often?

What support and services do the dealership offer after you buy the car?

Are there extra costs for installing a home charging station?

What driving conditions can affect the car's range the most? (Think about your lifestyle, like towing a trailer)

What safety features does the car have?

Does the car come with a charging cable?

Chapter 2. Choosing the Right EV for You

After the test drive

Reflect on your experience - Think about how the test drive went and if the car met your needs. Don't rush your decision or feel pressured to buy before you're ready.

Compare models - Look at how the car you tested stacks up against other electric cars in terms of features, price, and performance. Try driving a few other models to make a good comparison.

Consider costs - Think about the overall costs, including electricity, savings on fuel, maintenance, and any government incentives.

Check financing - Look into different ways to finance your car, like leasing or buying.

Plan for charging - Make sure you have a plan for charging your car at home. You might need to get a home charger installed before you can bring your new car home.

Next steps

If the car fits your needs, go ahead with the purchase.

If not, try other cars or rethink what you're looking for.

Electric Vehicles Explained

Chapter 2. Choosing the Right EV for You

CONCLUSION

In conclusion, buying an electric car is a big decision that needs careful thought and research. By asking the right questions, you'll understand how the car performs, what upkeep it needs, and any extra costs. Reflecting on your test drive and comparing different models will help you find the best one for your lifestyle. Also, think about overall costs like electricity, savings on fuel, upkeep, and any government incentives. Planning for home charging is crucial to making sure everything goes smoothly when you switch to an electric car. With this knowledge, you can confidently choose a car that fits your needs and daily activities. Remember, the right car should meet your expectations and make your life easier.

Chapter 3.
Easy Charging Basics

In our modern lives, electricity is essential, powering our homes and gadgets. Many things we use daily, like phones and computers, need batteries to work. These batteries have to be charged regularly. Even though we are used to charging our electronic devices, some people find it hard to understand how to charge an electric car. But the process is actually quite similar.

WHY EV'S NEED CHARGING

Electric vehicles run on electricity stored in their batteries, which powers the motor to make the car go. This means, just like any other device that needs batteries, EVs need to be charged often to keep them working and make sure they have enough power to drive well.

Hybrid vehicles generate their own electricity while driving, either through regenerative braking or an engine-driven generator. Plug-in hybrids work similarly but have a larger battery that can also be charged by plugging into the mains electricity.

A common concern for people considering electric vehicles (EVs) is that they can't charge their car at home, and that they would need to go to a charging station in order to use this type of car.

However, the same can be said for conventional vehicles, as a visit to a fuel station is necessary to fill the tank. As the EV infrastructure improves, it is likely that a charge point can be found closer to home than an equivalent fuel station, making it actually more convenient and practical.

Electric Vehicles Explained

Chapter 3.
Easy Charging Basics

Fully electric cars need electricity to run, which they get from their batteries. To charge these batteries, you need to connect the car to a power source. At home, you can plug your car into a regular electrical outlet, but the electricity needs to be changed from AC (alternating current) to DC (direct current) to be stored in the battery. This is done by the car's onboard charger, which also makes sure the battery charges correctly.

Charging an electric car means transferring electricity from a power source to the car's battery. You can do this in different ways, each with its own speed and convenience.

Charging is important for several reasons:

Range - Regular charging ensures your car has enough power for daily drives or longer trips without running out.

Battery health - Good charging habits, like not letting the battery completely run out and keeping it above a certain level, help the battery last longer and work better.

Convenience - Charging at home, work, or public stations gives you flexibility and makes it easier, so you don't need to stop often.

Keeping these points in mind will help you get the most out of your electric vehicle, making your experience smooth and enjoyable.

 Keeping your car's battery charged above 20% can help protect its health.

Electric Vehicles Explained

Chapter 3.
Easy Charging Basics

WHAT IS REGENERATIVE BRAKING?

Regenerative braking is a clever feature in electric cars that helps recharge the battery while the car is slowing down or stopping. It converts the energy used to slow the car into electricity, which is then stored back in the battery. This not only boosts the car's efficiency by using energy that would otherwise go to waste but also helps the car travel further on a single charge. It's an excellent way to make the most out of every drive.

Here's how it works:

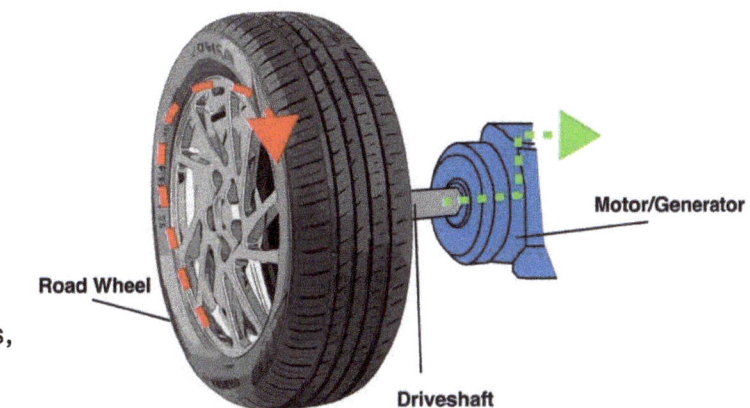

The science says energy cannot be created or destroyed, only changed from one form to another.

When a car moves, it has energy called kinetic or movement energy. To slowdown, this energy needs to turn into another type. In regular cars, when you press the brake pedal, this energy changes to heat through friction at the brake pads and discs, which slows the car. This heat energy is then lost to the air, which means we're wasting useful energy.

In an electric car, when you press the brake, instead of just using traditional brakes, the car's electric motor acts like a generator. It changes the car's movement energy back into electrical energy, slowing the car down.

Electric Vehicles Explained

Chapter 3.
Easy Charging Basics

The recovered electrical energy goes back to the battery, adding a bit more charge. This not only helps the car go further by reusing energy that would otherwise be lost, but it also reduces the wear on the braking system.

The benefits of regenerative braking for EVs are significant:

Energy efficiency - It reuses energy that would otherwise be wasted, making the vehicle more efficient overall.

Extended range - By capturing energy when you brake, the vehicle can go further on one charge.

Reduced brake wear - Because the system uses the electric motor to slow down the vehicle, the traditional brakes are used less often, which means lower maintenance costs and longer-lasting brakes.

It's worth remembering that regenerative braking has some limits.

It can only recover a small amount of energy, so you might not see a big boost in your battery charge.

It only works on the wheels connected to the motor, so regular brakes are needed for the other wheels.

Regenerative braking is less effective when driving slowly, so you'll still need conventional brakes.

And if your battery is fully charged, there's no place for the extra electricity to go, so the car will rely on its regular brakes.

Chapter 3.
Easy Charging Basics

ELECTRIC VEHICLE SUPPLY EQUIPMENT (EVSE) TERMINOLOGY

Before we dive into the details of EV charging, let's get to grips with some basic terms related to Electric Vehicle Supply Equipment (EVSE). These terms will make it easier to follow along and get the most out of your electric vehicle experience.

EVSE (Electric Vehicle Supply Equipment) - This is the whole system that provides electricity from a power source to an electric vehicle. It includes the plugs, cables, power outlets, and the communication systems needed to make sure charging is safe and efficient.

Connector - This is the part you plug into your electric vehicle to charge it. Different *'types'* of connectors are used for different charging speeds and car models.

Cable - This is the cord that carries electricity from the charging equipment to your car. It must match the plug and the car's charging socket.

Tethered/Untethered - This means whether the charging cable is always attached to the charging station. A tethered cable stays fixed to the charging station, while untethered means you have your own cable that you plug in-between the charging station and the car.

Charging station - A charging station is a place where you can fill up your electric car with power. It can be as simple as a wall-mounted unit at home, or a more complex system found in public places.

Charging port - Is where you plug in your electric car to charge it.

Electric Vehicles Explained

Chapter 3.
Easy Charging Basics

Kilowatts (KW) - This measures how quickly energy is transferred. For EV charging, it represents the power output of the charging station.

Kilowatt-hours (KWh) - Kilowatt-hours measure how much energy is used over time. Think of it like the fuel tank size in a regular car. It's a way to show how much power your EV's battery can store.

DC (Direct Current) and AC (Alternating Current) - These are two types of electrical currents used to charge electric vehicles. *Level 1* and *Level 2* chargers use AC, while *Level 3* chargers use DC.

Single and Three-Phase - Electricity can be supplied in two main ways: single-phase and three-phase. Think of single-phase as a single hose filling a bucket slowly and steadily, while three-phase is like using three hoses to fill the bucket much faster.

Single-phase electricity is what you usually find in homes and small businesses since it's simple and works well for everyday needs.

Three-phase electricity is used in larger buildings and factories. It's more powerful and efficient for running big machines or equipment that need a lot of energy. With three wires working together, three-phase electricity provides power smoothly and can handle higher loads without interruptions.

Electric Vehicles Explained

Chapter 3.
Easy Charging Basics

CHARGING LEVELS

There are three main ways to charge an electric vehicle, which differ in speed and convenience.

Level 1 charging - This is the slowest method, using a regular household socket. It adds about 3 to 5 miles of driving range per hour of charging. It's handy for overnight charging at home but not great for quick top-ups.

Level 2 charging - This type is faster and needs a special charger, usually installed at home or found in public places. It adds about 10 to 20 miles of range per hour and is a good balance between speed and convenience.

Level 3 charging (DC fast charging) - These are the fastest chargers, generally found at public charging stations. They can add about 60 to 80 miles of range in just 20minutes. However, not all EVs can use Level 3 chargers, so check your car's compatibility.

Each level has its own benefits and drawbacks. Don't worry if it seems a bit confusing at first - with a little practice, you'll soon get the hang of it. Just think about how you use your car and where you can charge it most conveniently. Whether at home, work, or while you're out and about, there's a charging solution that will work for you.

Two key terms are used to explain vehicle charging: Mode and Type; simply put:

Mode - describes how you charge your car, like slow, fast, or rapid, and whether it's using AC or DC power.

Type - refers to the shape of the plug and socket that connects your car to the charger.

Electric Vehicles Explained

Chapter 3.
Easy Charging Basics

Before you get a plug-in or electric vehicle, it's important to think about a few things. Do you have a driveway or garage where you can charge the car overnight? This is really handy for EV owners.

Be careful about running an electric cable across pavements or public areas to charge your car parked on the street. This can be dangerous and may not be allowed unless you get permission from your local authority.

MODES

There are four *'Modes'* to charge your electric vehicle (EV). Each method has its own characteristics, but don't worry, you don't need to memorise all the technical details. The best approach is to understand the basics and choose what works for you.

As charging technology keeps improving, the specific numbers and times will change, so it's more useful to focus on understanding the general concepts.

Mode 1 – Single or Three-Phase AC charging

Mode 1 is an early method for charging electric vehicles. It uses a simple extension lead that can be plugged into a regular home socket or a commercial power supply. This method does not have any smart communication with the car, and the only protection is the fuse in the plug or a circuit breaker. Think of it as a basic, somewhat outdated charging method. As a result, Mode 1 charging is rarely used today.

Electric Vehicles Explained

Chapter 3.
Easy Charging Basics

Mode 2 – Single or Three-Phase AC charging

Mode 2 is a step up from Mode 1 and can be used with a regular home electricity socket or a special three-phase connector. Unlike Mode 1, Mode 2 comes with a smart charging box (called an in-cable charging box ICCB) that lets the car, and the charger talk to each other and manage the charging process.

Because Mode 2 charges very slowly, some people call it 'granny charging' as it's like the gentle pace of a granny.

Many electric vehicles come with a Mode 2 charging cable, or you can buy one separately. This cable can be plugged into most home sockets and usually charges at a safe amperage, below the fuse rating. For instance, if the fuse is rated at 13amps, the charging will be around 10 amps. This makes it easy and safe to charge your EV at home without needing any special equipment.

It's important to make sure that the socket you use to charge your EV is in good condition and suitable for the job. Charging from a damaged or incorrect socket can overheat and cause a fire. Avoid using extension leads because they add extra wiring, which can overheat and be a fire risk. Coiled-up extension leads are especially dangerous as they can overheat and cause a fire.

Even though many Mode 2 charging cables are waterproof, don't let them sit in standing water or get submerged. Check the manufacturer's instructions for any specific advice.

Electric Vehicles Explained

Chapter 3.
Easy Charging Basics

Mode 3 – Single or Three-Phase AC charging

Mode 3 refers to any purpose-built/dedicated electric vehicle AC charging unit. Depending on its location and connection to the power grid, the capability for single or three-phase can be used. This means that dedicated equipment fitted to domestic residences will normally only have the capability to charge using the available single phase, however, if the equipment is fitted in a commercial environment, it may be able to deliver a three-phase charge. This gives a range of charging speeds from slow to fast. Mode 3 equipment may be tethered or untethered, referring to whether a charging lead is permanently fixed to the charging equipment. The advantage of using untethered equipment is that the vehicle owner may use an adapter to change the plug *type*, increasing the variety and style of vehicles that can be charged from a single unit.

Mode 3 chargers can come with a cable attached (tethered), while others don't (untethered).

If the cable isn't attached, you can use different adapters to fit various types of EVs.

This makes it super flexible and means you can charge different cars with the same charger, as long as you have the right adapter.

Electric Vehicles Explained

Chapter 3.
Easy Charging Basics

Mode 4 – DC rapid charging

Mode 4 is a special type of charger that gives your car a super-fast boost, sending power straight to the battery without needing to go through the car's regular charging system. It's like a turbocharger for your battery.

This type of charger can give your car an 80% boost in about 30 minutes. You usually won't find DC rapid chargers at home because they need a special kind of electricity supply. Instead, you'll see these chargers at key spots along highways or in cities. This setup helps with long trips and makes sure you don't worry about running out of battery.

Using a three-phase electrical supply, DC Chargers convert AC power to DC power before it reaches the vehicle. This allows for rapid charging, making it super-fast. The charging station connects to a commercial AC supply, changes the power to DC inside the unit, and then connects to the vehicle with a special DC cable and socket.

This type of charging is perfect for road trips, letting drivers quickly recharge their cars and get back on the road with little delay. Many electric car makers have set up networks of these fast-charging stations, making long-distance travel easier.

All level 3 chargers have cables fixed to the charging equipment because the system's safety and efficiency depend on these special components. The charging plug of a DC rapid charger has its own unique socket, which can be combined with the level 2 port or be a completely separate unit mounted next to it. This means drivers need to ensure the plug and socket match their EV and the charging station.

Electric Vehicles Explained

Chapter 3.
Easy Charging Basics

Charging speeds are often described by how much power they deliver:

Slow - 2.4 to 6 kW

Fast - 7 to 22 kW

Rapid - 25 to 100 kW

Ultra rapid - 100 to 350 kW

No matter which charging method you choose, the built-in charger in your electric vehicle will determine how fast the battery can charge.

This is because the charger is designed to protect the battery and ensure it lasts as long as possible.

So even if you plug your car into a super-fast charger, it will only charge at the maximum rate set by the car manufacturer.

This is a feature to make sure your battery stays healthy and safe.

Tesla Supercharger and Destination Charger

Tesla has a network of fast charging stations called Superchargers. These are designed mainly for Tesla electric cars and can provide a lot of power quickly. Tesla also has slower charging stations known as Destination chargers. These are often found at places like restaurants or hotels, where you might be doing something else while your car charges.

Chapter 3.
Easy Charging Basics

 When a vehicle is plugged into a charger, it's essential to remember that the system is still live, meaning electricity is flowing. Even though there are many safety systems in place to protect you, the high-voltage system cannot be completely turned off.

TYPES OF CHARGING PLUG AND SOCKET

When electric and hybrid cars first came out, there wasn't a standard way to design the charging sockets. This means different cars had different *'Types'* of sockets and plugs. Over time, some designs became more popular and are now used by many car makers. You'll need to know which *Type* of plug your car has so you can use the right charger.

All plugs have pins and sockets to let electricity flow and to allow the car and the charger to communicate with each other. The larger pins provide the power, while the smaller ones handle the communication.

The two smaller pins in the socket are known as the proximity pilot (PP) and control pilot (CP).

The proximity pilot (PP) has several important jobs.

- First, it tells the car that a charging cable is plugged in.
- Second, it informs the car's charger about the cable's size and charging capacity in amps.
- Lastly, it activates an immobiliser so the car can't be driven away while the charging cable is connected.

Electric Vehicles Explained

Chapter 3.
Easy Charging Basics

 On some socket designs, the proximity pilot pin is slightly longer than the control pilot, extending further out into the socket. This ensures that it is the first pin to make connection when plugged in and the last pin to disconnect when unplugging.

The control pilot (CP) is a way for the car and the charger to talk to each other. It helps them figure out if the car is ready to charge, how much power to send to the battery, and what stage of charging the car is in.

Type 1 – Yazaki

Type 1 charging connectors are mainly used by car designers and manufacturers in Asia and North America. This type can only work with single-phase AC electricity, up to 250 volts. It has three main power connections, meaning that it can only charge with single-phase AC electricity, no matter the supply available. It also includes the communication ports/pins needed for charging.

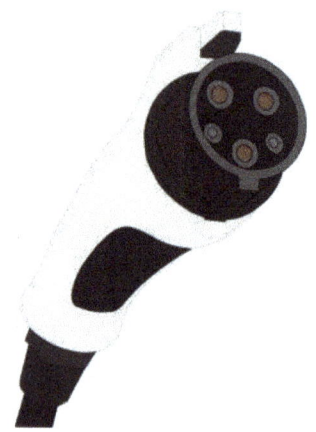

Electric Vehicles Explained

Chapter 3.
Easy Charging Basics

Type 2 – Mennekes

Type 2 charging connectors are mainly used by carmakers in Europe. They have five high-voltage connections, so they can charge using either single-phase or three-phase electricity. If you're using a single-phase supply, only three of the pins are needed. But if three-phase power is available, the extra two pins are used, which speeds up the charging process. These connectors also have the necessary communication ports.

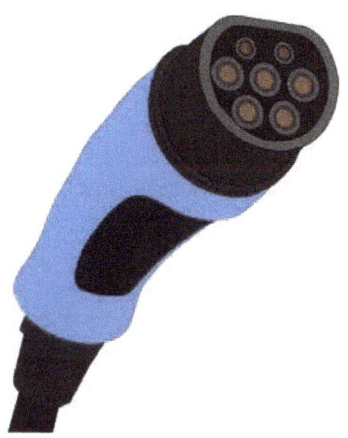

 Type 2 connectors are popular in Europe because they can easily switch between single-phase and three-phase electricity, making them flexible and efficient. European car manufacturers and designers prefer this type due to its versatility.

GB/T

In China, the official EV charging standard is known as GB/T. There are two types of connectors: one is similar to the European Type 2, and the other is used for rapid DC charging, called GB/T20234.3. This rapid charging connector has its own socket, usually placed next to the regular charging socket. It has large pins for the positive and negative direct current (DC), an earth connection for safety, and five smaller pins for communication with the charging station. This setup ensures a safe and efficient charging process, whether you're using regular or rapid charging.

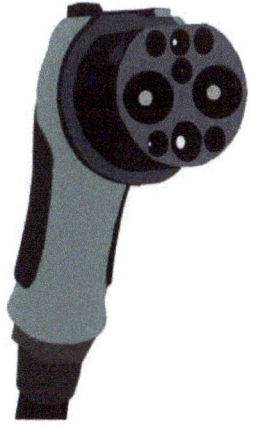

Electric Vehicles Explained

Chapter 3.
Easy Charging Basics

Type 3 – Scame

Type 3 charging connectors, once used widely in Europe, came in two versions: Type 3A for single-phase power and Type 3C for three-phase power. However, due to advancements and new standards, these types have become less common.

 In January 2013, the Type 2 connector became the official EV charging connector in Europe. This means that the older Type3 socket is mostly outdated and no longer used.

Type 4 – CHAdeMO

Type 4 charging connectors are mainly used in Asia and North America for fast charging. They have two pins for direct current (DC) charging and communication pins. CHAdeMO connectors are often paired with Type 1 connectors for AC charging, meaning vehicles with this setup have two separate sockets, usually side-by-side.

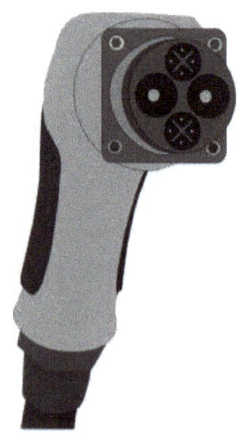

Electric Vehicles Explained

Chapter 3.
Easy Charging Basics

 CHAdeMO stands for "Charge de Move", or charge to move but also comes from a Japanese phrase meaning "how about a cup of tea?".

This phrase is used to suggest that charging your EV with a CHAdeMO connector takes about the same amount of time as brewing and drinking a cup of tea.

CCS Combined Charging Systems

To give manufacturers the flexibility to use both AC and DC fast charging with a simple socket design, there is the CCS or Combined Charging System. This system basically adds a two-pin DC socket below a Type 1 or Type 2 AC socket. This means your vehicle can use a Type 1 or 2 plug when only AC power is available, or a special plug that combines Type 1 or 2 with DC fast charging pins when DC power is available. For DC charging, only the **earth** pin for safety and the communication pins are needed in the AC socket.

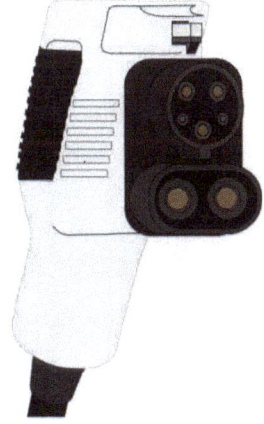 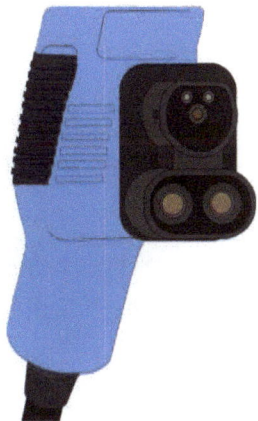

Electric Vehicles Explained

Chapter 3.
Easy Charging Basics

 **Earth** is a safety feature in electrical systems that directs excess electricity away from the appliance to prevent electric shocks.

NAS North American Standard

The NAS, also called the NACS (North American Charging System), is a type of plug developed by Tesla for charging electric cars. These plugs have been used in all Tesla cars sold in North America since 2012, and in November 2022, Tesla allowed other car makers to use them too. Some other car manufacturers have already decided to use the NAS plugs for their electric cars in North America.

NAS plugs have five pins. Two are used to charge the car quickly, and they can also charge it more slowly with regular electricity. There is an earth pin for safety, and other pins for communication.

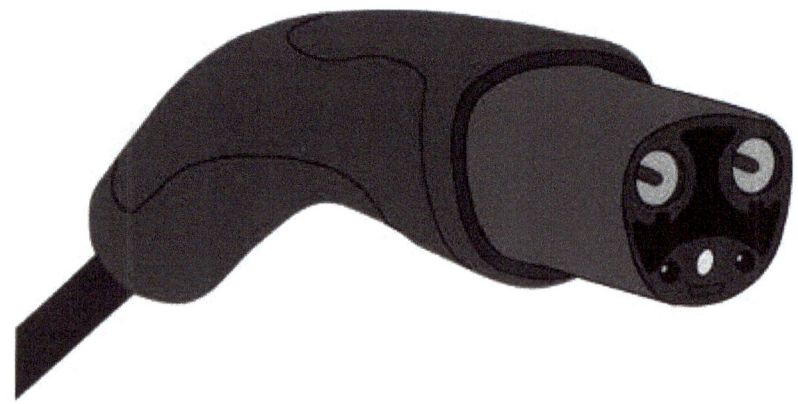

Electric Vehicles Explained

Chapter 3.
Easy Charging Basics

CHARGING AND EQUIPMENT

The availability and choice of charging stations are important for people considering electric vehicles. Knowing about different charging options helps new owners make good decisions. Whether you're planning to charge at home or use public stations, understanding how each type works will help you enjoy owning an electric car without stress.

To charge your electric car, you will need the right equipment and a power source. You can charge at home using household electricity or at public charging points.

Most public chargers will involve a fee, which can vary a lot. It's worth checking ahead to avoid surprises.

Public charging usually means paying as you go, so you'll need a way to pay for each session.

Many chargers now accept debit or credit cards, but some may need a special phone app or prepayment.

Planning ahead is key when you're going on a trip that might need a charging stop.

There are lots of mobile phone apps available that can help you locate public chargers.

Electric Vehicles Explained

Chapter 3.
Easy Charging Basics

Charging Level 1 – Mode 2

Step 1
- Make sure the main power supply is turned off before you start.

Step 2
- Check the charging cable and the in-cable charging box (ICCB) for any obvious damage or wear. If you spot any issues, don't plug it in and seek advice.

Step 3
- Connect the charging lead to the mains power and switch it on. The cable will usually check itself and show a sign on the ICCB if everything is working right. If there's a problem, turn off the power, unplug the cable, and get some help.

Step 4
- Some charging cables let you choose how fast they charge. You can set this now. (Slower charging is better for your battery in the long run, but it takes more time.) Your choice here depends on what you prefer and the type of car you have.

Step 5
- Open the vehicle's charging port. This might involve using a lever or switch, much like opening a fuel cap on a traditional car.

Step 6
- Make sure the charging lead isn't lying across a walkway where someone could trip over it. Firmly plug the lead into the vehicle's socket. This usually just means pushing the plug into the socket until it clicks into place.

Electric Vehicles Explained

Chapter 3.
Easy Charging Basics

Step 7

- Once the cable is plugged in, you should see a charging indicator light upon the charging box. Your car's dashboard will also show that it's charging, with a display similar to a fuel gauge, showing how much charge, you have and how long it will take to fully charge. It's normal to hear some clicks and noises from the car as it starts charging—these are just the electrical circuits turning on.

Step 8

- Many charging plugs lock into the socket to keep them from being unplugged unless you stop the charging first. With a Type 1 plug, you can press a trigger to stop the charging and disconnect the cable. This trigger often has a small hole where you can attach a padlock to prevent tampering.

Step 9

- You don't always need to fully charge the battery. If you have enough charge for your trip, you can stop the process whenever you like. To do this, you may need to unlock the car and press a button to stop charging.

Step 10

- When you're done charging, unplug the cable and close the charging flap on your car securely.

Step 11

- Turn off the main power supply, unplug the cable, and gently coil and store it.

Always follow the manufacturer's instructions.

Electric Vehicles Explained

Chapter 3.
Easy Charging Basics

Charging Level 2 – Mode 3

Step 1
- Park your vehicle close to the charger, making sure it's not blocking anyone or causing a hazard. A public charger might need you to pay first.

Step 2
- Check the charging cable and equipment for any obvious damage. If you see any, don't use it—get help instead.

Step 3
- Open the charging port on your car, just like you would a fuel cap. This might involve using a lever or switch inside the car.

Step 4
- Avoid laying the charge lead across walkways where someone could trip. Firmly plug it into your car's socket until it clicks in place.

Step 5
- Once plugged in, you should see a light on the charging box and an indication on your car's dashboard, showing its charging. You'll probably hearsome clicks and noises—that's normal as the circuits engage.

Step 6
- Many plugs lock into place to prevent unplugging until charging stops. Ifyou have a Type 1 plug, you can press a trigger to stop charging and disconnect. There's often a hole for a padlock to prevent tampering.

Electric Vehicles Explained

Chapter 3.
Easy Charging Basics

> **Step 7**
- If you have enough charge for your trip, you don't need to fully charge the battery. You can stop anytime by unlocking the car and pressing a button to stop charging.

> **Step 8**
- When you're done, unplug the cable and close your car's charging flap securely.

> **Step 9**
- Turn off the main power supply, unplug the cable, and gently coil and store it.

Always follow the manufacturer's instructions.

 Charging Level 3 - Mode 4

> **Step 1**
- Park your car near the charger, making sure it doesn't block access for others or create any hazards. Public chargers may require pre-payment at this point.

> **Step 2**
- Check the charging cable and equipment for any obvious damage. If you see any issues, do not use the cable and seek help.

> **Step 3**
- Open the charging cover on your car. This might be like opening a fuel flap on a regular car—using a lever or a button inside the car.

Electric Vehicles Explained

Chapter 3.
Easy Charging Basics

> **Step 4**
- Be careful not to leave the charging cable where someone could trip over it. Plug the cable into your car's charging socket. Usually, you just need to push the plug in firmly. Remember, this socket might be different from the one you use at home.

> **Step 5**
- After you plug it in, you'll see a charging indicator on the charger and your car's display. This will show you how much charge your car has, similar to a fuel gauge, and how much time is left to fully charge. Because fast charging is powerful, it usually stops at 80% to protect the battery and make it last longer. You might hear some clicks and noises as the charging starts—that's normal as the circuits engage.

> **Step 6**
- At this point, many charging plugs will lock into place to keep them secure.

> **Step 7**
- You don't have to fully charge the battery if there's enough range for your trip. You can stop the charging process whenever you want. To do this, you might need to unlock the car and press a button to stop charging.

> **Step 8**
- After unplugging, close and secure the charge flap on your car.

> **Step 9**
- Disconnect and carefully coil and store the charging cable.

Always follow the manufacturer's instructions.

Electric Vehicles Explained

Chapter 3.
Easy Charging Basics

Besides the main charging methods, new and exciting options are coming out in the electric vehicle world. One such innovation is wireless charging, which lets EVs charge without needing to plug in, similar to how mobile phones or electric toothbrushes do. This technology uses electromagnetic fields to transfer energy, making it a handy solution where space is tight, and convenience is key.

Benefits of wireless charging include:

- No cables required, reducing the risk of tripping over wires.
- Easy to use; just park your car near the charger, and it starts charging. You might not even need to get out of the car.
- As the technology gets better, it creates more chances to expand the charging network.

Other technology such as solar-powered charging stations are becoming more popular. They use renewable energy to charge electric vehicles, which is great for the environment and helps reduce our carbon footprint. This means we can enjoy the benefits of driving an EV while also supporting sustainability.

Electric Vehicles Explained

Chapter 3.
Easy Charging Basics

VEHICLE TO GRID (V2G) AND VEHICLE TO EVERYTHING (V2X)

Vehicle to Grid, or V2G, is a system where electric cars can not only charge up from the power grid but also give electricity back to it when needed. Imagine your car's battery acting like a giant power bank. During times when lots of people need power, your car can help out by supplying some of its stored energy. If lots of cars do this, it can make a big difference. It helps keep electricity costs down and may even earn you some money when you sell power back to the grid.

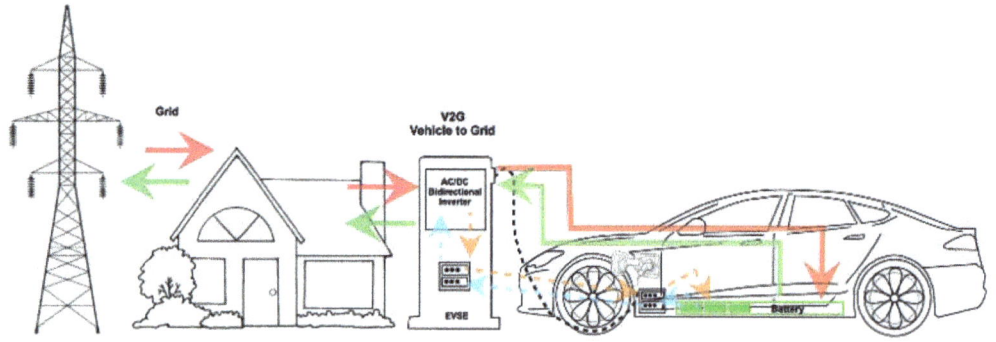

Vehicle-to-Everything, or V2X, takes things a step further. It means your electric car can talk to different systems around it to make everything run smoother and safer. For example, your car can chat with traffic lights to find the quickest route or talk to other cars to avoid crashes. It can even look out for pedestrians and help keep them safe. V2X promises to make our roads smarter and more connected, moving us towards a better, more sustainable future.

Chapter 3.
Easy Charging Basics

CONCLUSION

In summary, charging an electric vehicle (EV) has become much easier with clear instructions and new technologies. By following simple steps, any EV owner can confidently plug in their car and recharge their battery. Keeping an eye on the charging indicators and knowing the best charge levels will help keep the battery healthy and make sure energy is used efficiently.

The future of EV charging is exciting, with new ideas like wireless charging, which means no more cables, and solar-powered stations that are great for the environment. Beginners can feel at ease knowing that managing an EV's charge is not only easy but also part of a bigger move towards smart and green transportation. Learning these basics now will prepare you for the eco-friendly technologies of the future.

Chapter 4. Driving an EV: Tips for Beginners

For those new to electric cars, getting to grips with how to drive and operate these vehicles can seem daunting at first. This chapter aims to make that transition easier by offering practical tips and habits to help beginners start driving an EV. From unlocking and entering the car to starting and driving it smoothly, each step will be simplified for your ease.

Driving an EV is a unique experience compared to traditional petrol/gasoline or diesel cars. One major difference is the quiet start, as EVs run almost silently. Additionally, features like preheating or cooling the car before you drive can enhance your comfort and save energy. Whether you're planning short commutes or long trips, these basic tips will ensure you're well-prepared to enjoy the benefits of your electric vehicle.

RANGE

Range refers to how far an electric car can go on a fully charged battery. Think of the range as similar to the fuel gauge in a conventional car. It shows you how much distance you can cover before needing a recharge.

Chapter 4. Driving an EV
Tips for Beginners

This estimate can change based on several factors, such as:

- How you drive
- The weather
- The weight of the car
- If you're towing anything
- Tyre pressure

Most daily trips are easily manageable on a full battery, but it's important to check your range before starting longer journeys. Planning where to stop and recharge can help avoid running out of power.

Modern EV batteries don't need to be fully run down before recharging. You can top up the battery whenever you have the chance or even stop partway through a journey to add a bit more charge and ease any worries about running out.

Range anxiety' is a common concern for new electric vehicle drivers. It refers to the fear or worry that your car's battery will runout of power before you reach your destination or a charging point.

This anxiety can be similar to the feeling of running low on fuel in a traditional vehicle but is often heightened due to the fewer available charging stations when compared to fuel stations.

Electric Vehicles Explained

Chapter 4. Driving an EV: Tips for Beginners

ACCES AND ENTRY

Getting into and starting an electric vehicle is easy, even for beginners.

Key fob or app

Many electric vehicles come with a key fob or a mobile phone app that you can use to unlock the car. Just press the unlock button on the key fob or follow the instructions on the app to open the car. Some manufacturers use a credit card-sized key card, which you need to hold against the car's body in a specific spot to unlock it. Check your vehicle's manual for detailed instructions.

Proximity sensors

Some electric vehicles will unlock automatically when the key fob or card is close by. Check if your car does this by approaching it and see if the doors unlock without pressing any buttons.

To stay safe, keep your key fob or card in a secure place where it can't accidentally unlock your car. This helps prevent thieves from easily getting into your vehicle. Some thieves use a trick called "relay theft" to boost the signal from your key and unlock the car even if you're inside your house. A Faraday pouch is a small bag or box you can use to keep your keys in when you're at home. It blocks radio signals, helping to prevent theft.

Electric Vehicles Explained

Chapter 4. Driving an EV
Tips for Beginners

Door handles

To improve the look and make the car more streamlined, some electric vehicles have door handles that sit flush with the door when not in use. Depending on the model, the handles might pop out or light up when you're ready to use them. Simply pull the handle like you would on any other car.

Entering the vehicle

Once the car is unlocked, open the door, get in, and adjust the driver's seat. You can move it forward and back, and some seats even go up and down. Some might also have an option for supporting your lower back.

In some EVs, you can adjust the steering wheel's position too. Make sure you can reach the pedals and steering wheel comfortably, with your arms slightly bent.

Next, adjust all mirrors or cameras to ensure you have the best view around the car. Take a moment to look at the dashboard and controls to get familiar with them.

Proper seating position in a car is not just about comfort but also crucial for safety. One of the key aspects is the proximity to the steering wheel airbag. Airbags are designed to deploy rapidly in the event of a collision, providing a cushion between the driver and the steering wheel or dashboard. However, if the driver is seated too close to the steering wheel, the force of the airbag deployment can cause serious injury. The steering wheel should be aimed at the chest, not the face, which can be achieved by adjusting the steering column if the vehicle has that feature. This positioning minimises the risk of head and neck injuries in the event of an airbag deployment.

Electric Vehicles Explained

Chapter 4. Driving an EV: Tips for Beginners

Start-up

Most EVs start with a simple press of a button, often without the need for a placing key in the ignition like you would on a conventional car. Make sure your foot is on the brake pedal when you press the start button. The car will start up silently, so you will need to check dashboard indications to see that the vehicle is ready to drive. (see silent start). To switch off, make sure the drive selector is in park with your foot on the brake pedal; press the start button again to power down. Check the dashboard to see that the car is switched off.

Never leave the car turned on and ready to drive while unattended.

Once the car is in ready mode, it can move if accidentally shifted into drive, so always be extra careful.

Preheat/Cool

Many electric cars have a handy feature that lets you heat or cool the inside of the car before you start driving. This ensures the car is comfortable, no matter the weather. You can also use this feature to defrost the windows ahead of time, so your car is ready to drive with clear visibility.

Using both the air conditioning and heater together can help clear mist from the windows faster.

This combination removes moisture from the air, making it easier to see out of your windows.

Electric Vehicles Explained

Chapter 4. Driving an EV Tips for Beginners

Using the mobile app

Many EVs come with a mobile app that lets you control different features, including climate settings, from your phone. Open the app, find the climate control or preconditioning option, and set the temperature you want. You can also turn on the heating or cooling system before you leave home. This may include using heated or cooled seats, ensuring your car is comfortable when you get in.

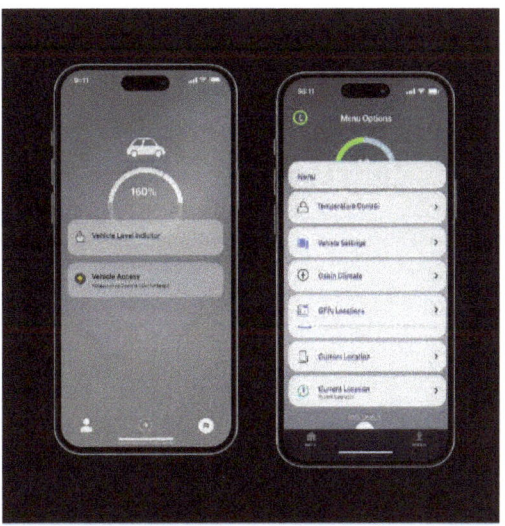

Scheduled preconditioning

Some EVs allow you to schedule preconditioning. This means you can set a specific time for the car to start heating or cooling automatically. This feature is particularly useful if you have a regular schedule, such as leaving for work at the same time every day. This may require you to familiarise yourself with the vehicle's touchscreen interface.

Manual activation

If you don't have access to the mobile app or prefer manual control, you can usually activate the climate control from within the vehicle. Enter the car and use the touchscreen or climate control buttons to set your preferred temperature.

Electric Vehicles Explained

Chapter 4. Driving an EV: Tips for Beginners

 Preheating or cooling your car while it's still plugged in can help save battery power, as the energy used comes from the charging source rather than the car's battery.

Therefore, if you have access to home charging, climate preconditioning can be achieved without affecting your potential driving range.

Silent start

Electric vehicles are designed to start very quietly, often without the noise associated with traditional internal combustion engines. This silent operation can sometimes make it difficult to tell if the car is actually switched on.

Here's how you can check that your car is ready to go:

Dashboard indicators - When you press the start button (usually while keeping your foot on the brake pedal), look at the dashboard. There should be a light or message indicating that the car is "Ready" or "On."

Instrument panel lights - You might also see the instrument panel lights up, showing various symbols and information about the car's status. Be aware of any warning symbols that stay on when the car is in ready mode.

Subtle sounds - While the engine might be silent, you may hear other subtle sounds, such as the hum of the climate control system or the faint noise from the electric motor.

By paying attention to these indicators, you can confidently know that your EV is started and ready to drive.

Chapter 4. Driving an EV
Tips for Beginners

 If the EV is a hybrid, the engine will stop and start as needed. So, the car engine might start suddenly. This could happen because of driving conditions or the need to charge the battery. Usually, the vehicle decides this on its own, not the driver.

 Always keep an eye on any warnings that show up on the dashboard.

If you see any warning lights while you're driving, find a safe place to stop and get some help.

Touchscreen and stalks

Most EVs feature a central touchscreen that controls various functions, including navigation, entertainment, climate control, and vehicle settings.

 Additionally, stalks behind the steering wheel manage essential functions like turning signals, windscreen wipers, and headlights. Take time to learn how to use and access the features included with the design of your electric car. Never make physical adjustments to any touchscreen settings while the vehicle is in motion.

Electric Vehicles Explained

Chapter 4. Driving an EV: Tips for Beginners

Noise generators

Electric vehicles are remarkably quiet, which can sometimes pose a risk to pedestrians who might not hear them approaching. To address this concern, EV manufacturers have incorporated noise generators that produce artificial sounds to alert pedestrians, especially in urban areas or car parks. These noise generators help ensure safety while maintaining the vehicle's quiet operation.

Noise generators in EVs are designed to emit sounds at low speeds, typically below 12 miles per hour (MPH) or 20 kilometres per hour (KPH). When the car is moving slowly, it produces specific noises designed by the manufacturer often resembling a light humming. As the car accelerates and reaches higher speeds, the noise generator usually turns off, as the tyre and wind noise become sufficient for pedestrians to hear.

Most electric cars have the option to switch off the noise generator, which could potentially lead to an accident.

Unless there is a specific need, always leave the noise generator switched on.

Remember that once in ready mode the car is live and if accidently placed in drive for example, could move without warning.

Electric Vehicles Explained

Chapter 4. Driving an EV Tips for Beginners

DRIVER CONTROLS

Driving an electric vehicle is similar in many ways to driving a conventional automatic car. However, there are differences that the driver should take time to learn or consider.

Once ready, a drive mode can now be selected in a similar manner to that used in a traditional automatic transmission. With your foot on the brake pedal, a leaver, knob or switch can be used to select the desired drive mode. This will often be labelled:

D - Drive, for normal forward motion.

R - Reverse, used when backing up.

P - Park, used to lock and hold the vehicle when stationary.

N - Neutral, used to allow the vehicle to roll freely (should not be used instead of park).

B - Braking or battery, used to increase or decrease the amount of regenerative braking available in drive modes on some cars.

Electric Vehicles Explained

Chapter 4. Driving an EV: Tips for Beginners

Park

When you want to stop and secure your EV, you need to shift the gear selector to the Park (P) position. This locks the transmission, preventing the car from moving. The parking brake should also be applied.

Accelerator and brake

Just like in conventional cars, EVs have an accelerator pedal to speed up and a brake pedal to slow down. However, EVs offer smooth and instant acceleration due to their electric motors, making driving more responsive. Care should be taken to learn the 'feel' of the driving experience when using the accelerator and brake.

When you press the accelerator pedal, the electric motor responds immediately, giving you a quick and powerful start. This instant power can make driving more fun and dynamic.

However, this quick response time might take some getting used to if you're accustomed to traditional engine powered cars. With practice, you'll learn to adjust your driving style to take full advantage of this feature.

Driving modes

EVs often come with different driving modes, such as Economy (Eco) and Sport. In Eco mode, the car prioritises energy efficiency, helping you to extend your battery range. This is ideal for longer trips or when you want to conserve power. In Sport mode, the car delivers maximum performance and responsiveness, which can be exciting for a more spirited driving experience.

Electric Vehicles Explained

Chapter 4. Driving an EV Tips for Beginners

REGENERATIVE BRAKING

When you lift your foot off the accelerator, the car slows down and recharges the battery. It might feel unusual at first but is easy to adapt to.

Regenerative braking is a feature in electric cars that helps to recharge the battery while you drive.

As the car slows down, the electric drive motor acts as a generator and converts some of the car's kinetic (movement) energy into electrical energy. This energy is then directed to the car's battery for later use.

So, in simple terms, regenerative braking helps you save energy and extend your driving range by turning some of the car's slowing-down energy into usable battery power.

B Modes

Some electric cars come with a 'B' mode, which stands for 'Brake' or 'Battery.' This mode enhances the regenerative braking system, allowing you to recover more energy while slowing down, thus extending your driving range.

Drivers of vehicles with an internal combustion engine should be familiar with the effect of **engine braking**. This is where the driver takes their foot off the accelerator and instead of the engine driving the wheels, the wheels try and drive the engine. Due to internal loads created inside the engine, this has the effect of slowing the vehicle down. With engine driven hybrid cars, this would reduce the efficiency of the kinetic (movement) energy recovery and any regenerative braking. Therefore, when decelerating the engine is often decoupled or operated in a manner that reduces its ability to provide engine braking.

Electric Vehicles Explained

Chapter 4. Driving an EV: Tips for Beginners

With a fully electric vehicle, there is no engine in the first place to provide engine braking, meaning that any slowing down when the drivers foot is taken off the accelerator comes from the **kinetic energy** recovery of the drive motor/generators.

Lots of electric car models are able to electronically vary the amount of **regeneration** using something called 'B' mode. This can often be found on the gear selection or may have separate switches or paddles by the steering wheel. B mode will allow the driver to select the scale of regeneration depending on personal preference or driving condition.

Based on the make and model, many cars will allow the kinetic energy recovery to be turned down to almost nothing, meaning that the vehicle **freewheels** when the accelerator is released. This can be a good method for economy as it might reduce the number of times the driver has to apply the accelerator to maintain speed. In this mode, much of any slowing down required will come from the standard hydraulic/friction braking system.

Chapter 4. Driving an EV
Tips for Beginners

If B mode is increased to the maximum, the car might act like it has a one pedal drive mode. When the throttle is pressed, the car will accelerate, and when released, the car will immediately slow down. This may sometimes be a helpful method of decent control when driving down long steep hills.

In any B mode, the hydraulic brakes should be used as normal by the driver to make up for any difference in slowing down or stopping required. Never rely solely on regenerative braking to act as the vehicles only method of deceleration.

The car can now be driven like a conventional automatic, however, remember that if the regenerative braking system (B mode) is turned up high it might almost act as a one pedal operation.

Engine braking is when a car slows down because the engine resists the motion, usually by the driver taking their foot off the accelerator.

Kinetic energy is the energy that an object has because it is moving. The faster an object moves, the more kinetic energy it has.

Regeneration is the process where an electric car converts some of its motion back into electricity to recharge the battery when slowing down.

Freewheel means to let a vehicle move by itself, without pressing the accelerator or using the brakes.

Electric Vehicles Explained

Chapter 4. Driving an EV: Tips for Beginners

DRIVING EFFICIENTLY IN AN ELECTRIC VEHICLE – TIPS FOR BEGINNERS

Electric vehicles offer a unique driving experience and come with features that can help you save energy and extend your battery life. By driving efficiently, you can maximise your car's range and enjoy an eco-friendly ride.

Here are some simple tips to help you get started:

Use Eco mode - Many electric cars have an Economy (Eco) mode that automatically prioritises energy efficiency while driving. When you activate Eco mode, the car adjusts its settings to conserve battery power. This can be ideal for longer trips or when you want to get the most out of your battery.

Maintain a steady speed - Try to avoid sudden acceleration and hard braking. Instead, try to maintain a steady speed. Smooth driving uses less energy and helps keep your battery charged for longer.

Plan your routes - Before you set off, plan your route to avoid heavy traffic and steep hills, if possible. These conditions can drain your battery faster. Using navigation apps that show traffic patterns and alternative routes can be helpful in finding the most energy-efficient path. If you require a charging stop, many navigation systems can add this to your route for you.

Use regenerative braking - Regenerative braking is a great feature in electric cars that helps recharge the battery. With practice, this process helps extend your driving range and reduces wear on the brake pads.

Chapter 4. Driving an EV Tips for Beginners

Monitor your battery - Keep an eye on your battery level (**state of charge**) and try to charge it regularly. Avoid letting it drop too low, as frequent **deep discharges** can shorten the battery's lifespan. Charging little and often can be more beneficial.

Use accessories wisely - Accessories like air conditioning, heating, and entertainment systems can sometimes use a lot of energy. Try to use them sparingly when battery charge is low or driving range/distance is a factor.

By following these simple tips, you can drive your electric vehicle more efficiently, save energy, and extend the life of your battery.

State of charge is the amount of battery power left in an electric car. It tells you how much energy is stored and available for use.

Deep discharge means using almost all of the battery's power before recharging it. This can sometimes shorten the battery's lifespan if done frequently.

CONCLUSION

Driving an electric car may seem daunting at first, but with a few simple tips, it becomes an easy and enjoyable experience. By using features such as Eco Mode and regenerative braking, maintaining a steady speed, and planning routes efficiently, beginners can maximise their car's range and battery life. Once familiar with these practices, driving an EV becomes second nature, offering a smooth, eco-friendly alternative to conventional vehicles.

Electric Vehicles Explained

Chapter 5.
Navigating Range Anxiety

Range anxiety is a term used to describe the fear that an electric vehicle (EV) will run out of battery power before reaching its destination or a charging station. This concern is common among new EV drivers who are unsure about the vehicle's range and the availability of charging infrastructure, especially when they are used to the convenience of fuel stations.

However, the notion of range anxiety is often exaggerated. Modern electric vehicles have significantly improved their battery technology and can typically travel between 150 to 300 miles on a single charge, which is more than enough for most daily commutes and activities.

Many drivers initially worry about running out of battery, but once they start using their EVs, they find that the lifestyle is quite manageable. In fact, if owners have access to home charging and can fill their battery overnight, they tend to be easier to manage than their conventionally fuelled equivalents.

Chapter 5.
Navigating Range Anxiety

AVERAGE DAILY JOURNEY/USE

Understanding the average daily journey distance is crucial for electric vehicle users to manage range anxiety effectively. On average, most drivers travel between 20 to 40 miles per day. This distance is well within the capability of modern EVs, most of which offer ranges exceeding 150 miles on a single charge.

This means that for the vast majority of daily commutes, an electric vehicle can easily handle the journey without requiring a recharge. Also, advancements in battery technology and the increasing availability of public charging stations continue to enhance the convenience of using EVs for daily transportation.

 It's worth noting that urban driving tends to consume less battery power compared to motorway or highway driving due to lower speeds and frequent stops, which allow for regenerative braking to be more effective.

To maximise the efficiency and convenience of your electric car, it's essential to plan ahead and make informed decisions about your journey.

Here are some strategies to help you do just that:

Now your vehicle's range - The first step in planning your trip is to understand the range of your electric vehicle. Rember that manufacturer quoted range is often the best-case scenario and real-world figures will often be considerably less. The actual range will vary based on factors such as driving style, terrain, weather conditions, and the use of heating or air conditioning.

Electric Vehicles Explained

Chapter 5.
Navigating Range Anxiety

> The information on the car's dashboard indicating expected range will be an estimate based on previous trips, usage and driving style.
>
> Therefore, it is common for the displayed value to vary considerably as its data is updated in real time as the car is driven. This has led to the gauge to sometimes be referred to as the 'guess-ometer'.

Use navigation tools - Most electric cars are equipped with sophisticated navigation systems that can assist you in planning routes. Many systems often feature built-in capabilities to locate charging stations along your planned route. Make use of these tools to identify where you can recharge if necessary.

Use smartphone apps - There are several smartphone applications designed to help EV drivers. These apps can provide real-time data on the locations of charging stations, their availability, and the *Types* of connectors they support. These apps can be invaluable in ensuring you have access to charging points when needed.

Plan for charging stops - When embarking on longer journeys, plan your route with charging stops in mind. Knowing where you can charge your vehicle will help reduce anxiety and ensure a smooth trip.

Electric Vehicles Explained

Chapter 5.
Navigating Range Anxiety

 It's a good idea to have a backup charging station identified in case your first choice is unavailable or occupied.

Optimise your driving style - Developing efficient driving habits can significantly extend your EV's range. Smooth acceleration and deceleration, maintaining a steady speed, and minimising the use of climate control systems will help conserve battery power. Additionally, take advantage of regenerative braking whenever possible.

 It is not unusual for new EV drivers to quickly adapt their driving technique to a more efficient style.

The dashboard display of many electric cars shows real-time efficiency values, sometimes in the form of animations.

The competitive nature of many drivers can lead to a change in driving habits as they try and improve their personal efficiency over previous trips. This 'efficiency game' often has the subconscious side-effect of retraining driving styles and improving range.

Charge at home - If you have the capability to charge your car at home, do so overnight. This can take advantage of cheaper energy tariffs and ensures that you start each day with a full battery, providing maximum range for your daily activities.

Electric Vehicles Explained

Chapter 5.
Navigating Range Anxiety

Long charging times are often cited by electric vehicle detractors, because depending on available charging speeds, battery state of charge and onboard charger restrictions, it may take several hours to achieve a full charge.

However, if overnight charging is available the battery can be filled while you sleep, so charge times become irrelevant.

The only time needed is plugging in when you arrive home and unplugging before you begin your journey.

You can start each day with a fully charged battery; whereas nobody fills the fuel tank of a traditional vehicle on your driveway as you sleep.

By following these practical tips, you can effectively manage your car's range and ensure a more enjoyable and stress-free driving experience.

BATTERY SIZE AND CONSUMPTION

Electric vehicle batteries are measured in kilowatt-hours (KWh), which indicates the amount of energy the battery can store. Think of it like the size of your car's fuel tank; the larger the battery (measured in KWh), the more energy it can hold, and the further your car can travel on a single charge. For example, a typical EV might have a battery size of 60 KWh, giving it a range of approximately 200-250 miles, depending on driving conditions. However, these figures are continually improving as advancements in operating and battery technology develops.

Chapter 5.
Navigating Range Anxiety

Kilowatt-Hours vs. Miles Per Gallon

In conventional vehicles, fuel efficiency is often measured in miles per gallon (MPG) - how many miles a car can travel on one gallon of fuel. In EVs, we use kilowatt-hours per 100 miles (KWh/100 miles) to measure efficiency. To compare, think of KWh like the energy content in a gallon of petrol/gasoline. For example, if an electric car uses 30 KWh to travel 100 miles, it's similar to a conventional car using 3 gallons of fuel to travel the same distance.

A simple way to calculate equivalence is to use the conversion that 1 gallon of petrol/gasoline is roughly equal to 33.7 KWh of energy. So, if an EV uses 30KWh/100 miles, it's like getting approximately 113 MPG in a traditional car (33.7KWh/gallon divided by 30 KWh/100 miles).

DRIVE MOTOR POWER AND BATTERY CONSUMPTION

The power of an EV's drive motor impacts how quickly it consumes battery energy. Remember that power relates to how hard something is working.

Driving faster or accelerating quickly will use more power, like how a traditional car burns more fuel when driven aggressively. Also, using the heater, air conditioning, driving up hills or towing also increases energy consumption.

Electric Vehicles Explained

Chapter 5.
Navigating Range Anxiety

State of Charge (SoC)

State of Charge (SoC) shown on the dashboard, is the equivalent of a fuel gauge in a traditional vehicle. It indicates the remaining useable energy in the battery, normally shown as a percentage. For example, if your battery is at 70% SoC, it means you have 70% of the battery capacity available for use. Monitoring SoC helps you plan journeys and charging stops effectively to avoid running out of power.

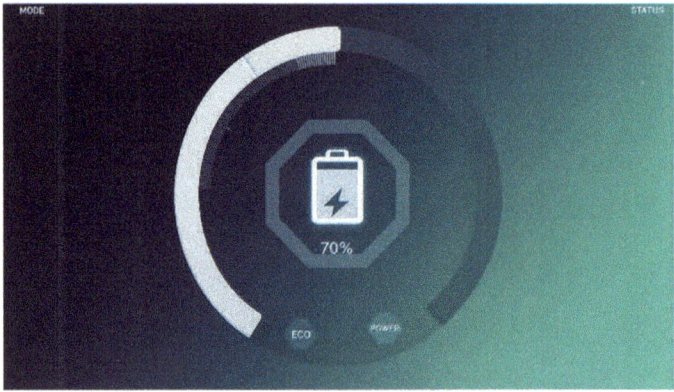

While manufacturers provide range estimates based on standardised tests, real-world conditions will affect these numbers. Factors such as driving style, weather, terrain, and use of electronic features can impact the actual range. For instance, cold weather can considerably reduce battery efficiency, lowering the range you can achieve on a full charge.

Battery aging and State of Health (SoH)

Over time, all batteries age and their capacity to hold charge diminishes. This is referred to as the battery's State of Health (SoH). This is a measure of a battery's ability to store and deliver energy compared to when it was new. For instance, after several years of use, an EV battery might retain 85-90% of its original capacity.

Chapter 5.
Navigating Range Anxiety

An analogy that can be used to explain the aging and state of health (SoH) of a battery is to liken it to the use of an electric kettle. The kettle uses electrical resistance in an element to convert electrical energy into heat, which can be used to boil water.

When an electric kettle is brand new, it will be the most efficient and effective as it will ever be at boiling water. Boil the kettle several hundred or thousand times and a scale from minerals in the water will begin to form around the element and on the inside walls of the kettle. Over time, this scale will reduce the efficiency of the heating element and the overall capacity of the kettle itself. A similar thing happens to the effectiveness of the battery every time itis charged and discharged.

While this means the range might decrease slightly, advancements in battery technology and proper maintenance can reduce these effects. For example, avoiding extreme temperatures, not consistently charging to 100%, and using moderate driving habits can prolong battery life.

Understanding EV batteries is crucial for maximising their benefits. With proper knowledge and management, you can enjoy the efficiency, cost savings, and environmental benefits that electric vehicles offer. Whether it's planning for your daily commutes or long trips, being informed will help you make the most out of your EV.

Electric Vehicles Explained

Chapter 5.
Navigating Range Anxiety

DRIVING STYLE

Driving style plays a significant role in how efficiently your electric vehicle uses its battery. Just like with traditional engine cars, driving habits can greatly influence your vehicle's range and overall performance.

Moderate acceleration and speed

Gentle acceleration and maintaining a steady, moderate speed can help conserve battery power. Rapid acceleration and high speeds require more energy, just as they would consume more fuel in conventional car. By accelerating smoothly and avoiding sudden stops, you can extend your EV's range considerably.

Use of accessories

Using accessories such as the air conditioning or heater also impacts the rate of battery consumption. These systems draw from the battery, reducing the overall range. Plan ahead and use these features carefully to manage energy usage better.

Electric Vehicles Explained

Chapter 5.
Navigating Range Anxiety

Regenerative braking

Most EVs come equipped with regenerative braking systems, which capture some of the energy typically lost during braking and feed it back into the battery. By anticipating traffic conditions and using regenerative braking effectively, you can recapture energy and increase your vehicle's range.

Terrain and driving conditions

Hilly terrain and stop-and-go traffic can affect your battery range as well. Climbing steep hills requires more power, while descending can actually help recharge the battery through regenerative braking. Similarly, city driving often involves frequent stops and starts which can be managed with careful driving to maximise efficiency.

By understanding these factors and adjusting your driving style accordingly, you can optimise your EV's performance and enjoy a longer, more efficient drive.

Electric Vehicles Explained

Chapter 5.
Navigating Range Anxiety

ALWAYS BE CHARGING (ABC)

Lithium-Ion batteries and memory effect

A common misconception with electric vehicles is that the battery needs to be rundown low before it can be recharged. This idea possibly stems from our experience of the advice given when charging batteries in older electronic equipment.

One of the significant advantages of modern electric vehicles is the use of lithium-ion batteries. Unlike older battery types found in consumer electronics, such as nickel-cadmium (NiCd) batteries, lithium-ion batteries do not suffer from a phenomenon known as memory effect.

Memory effect occurs when a battery "remembers" a lesser capacity if it is repeatedly charged after being partially discharged. This was a common issue with older batteries, where users needed to completely drain the battery before recharging to maintain its full capacity.

Lithium-ion batteries, however, are not affected by this. This means you can plug in your EV and top up the charge at any time without damaging the battery or reducing its capacity. In fact, it is potentially beneficial for your battery to be kept charged beyond a lower limit. This flexibility is incredibly convenient and helps ensure that your vehicle is always ready for use.

Electric Vehicles Explained

Chapter 5.
Navigating Range Anxiety

It's advisable to take advantage of charging facilities whenever they are available. By keeping your battery topped up, you can avoid running into low charge situations and ensure that you have sufficient range for your travels. This practice, often summarised as "Always Be Charging" (ABC), is a good habit for EV owners to adopt, ensuring that your car is ready for use.

Realistic usage

When it comes to using your electric vehicle, it's important to understand how driving conditions can affect battery consumption. Generally, city driving tends to use less battery power than motorway or highway driving.

With city driving, you often drive at lower speeds and encounter frequent stops at traffic lights and junctions. These conditions allow your EV to take advantage of regenerative braking, which helps to recharge the battery during braking. Additionally, the lower speeds mean less energy is required to maintain movement, and when stationary very little energy is used.

Chapter 5.
Navigating Range Anxiety

If your car is a hybrid, the engine usually turns off when you're not moving, which also helps to save fuel.

On the other hand, motorway or highway driving typically involves higher speeds and steady acceleration, which require more energy from the battery. At higher speeds, the battery has to work harder to overcome air resistance and maintain the vehicle's speed, leading to faster depletion of battery power.

Plan your trips more efficiently and make the most out of your EV's battery capacity.

CONCLUSION

In summary, driving smartly — like using accessories wisely, taking advantage of regenerative braking, and being aware of the terrain — along with planning your trips well, are crucial steps for overcoming range anxiety and getting the best performance from your electric vehicle.

Chapter 6.
Maintenance Made Simple

Routine maintenance for fully electric cars differs significantly from that of traditional vehicles. With the exception of hybrids, this is primarily due to the absence of a complex internal combustion engine.

One of the most notable differences is the absence of oil changes. Electric vehicles do not have an internal combustion engine that requires engine oil for lubrication. This means that EV owners are free from the regular oil change maintenance that is necessary for traditional vehicles. Additionally, EVs require fewer fluids overall; there's less need for **transmission** fluid, and brake fluid stress is reduced due to regenerative braking systems that help extend the life of brake components.

EVs lack an exhaust system entirely. Traditional vehicles rely on exhaust systems to manage the byproduct of burning fuel, which includes harmful emissions. EVs, on the other hand, produce no tailpipe emissions, eliminating the need for **silencers/mufflers**, **catalytic converters**, and exhaust pipes. This not only simplifies the maintenance process but also significantly reduces the environmental impact of the vehicle.

However, to ensure optimal performance and longevity, electric vehicles do require a regular maintenance. This involves routine checks and services that focus on key components such as the battery, tyres, brakes, heating cooling and ventilation (air conditioning) and software updates. Understanding these requirements can help owners avoid costly repairs and enhance the driving experience.

Chapter 6.
Maintenance Made Simple

The **transmission** is a part of a car that helps control how power is sent from the engine or drive motor to the wheels, allowing the vehicle to change speeds smoothly.

Silencers, also known as **mufflers**, are parts of a car's exhaust system that help reduce the noise created by the engine. They make the car quieter when it runs.

A **catalytic converter** is a part of a car that helps reduce harmful emissions by turning dangerous gases produced by the engine into less harmful ones before they leave the exhaust.

EV HIGH-VOLTAGE COMPONENTS AND THEIR PURPOSE

To help understand the operation of an electric car, it might be useful to know what some of the main components do.

High voltage drive battery

The high voltage drive battery is the power source of an electric car, similar to a fuel tank in traditional vehicles. It stores energy and supplies it to the electric motor, making the car go.

Electric Vehicles Explained

Chapter 6.
Maintenance Made Simple

Unlike regular car batteries that use 12 volts, the battery in an electric car can use hundreds of volts, storing a lot more energy. It's often found under the car in a protective case and is made up of many smaller **cells** that combine to create the high voltage needed.

There are two main types of batteries used: older hybrid cars often used **nickel metal hydride (Ni-MH)** batteries, but most modern electric cars use **lithium-ion (Li-ion)** batteries. Li-ion batteries are great because they're lightweight and can store a lot of energy in a small space.

Just like any battery, these don't last forever and need to be recharged regularly to keep your car running smoothly.

Electric Vehicles Explained

Chapter 6.
Maintenance Made Simple

 High voltages are very dangerous, and accidental contact can cause serious injury or even death. Never touch, take apart, or work on any electric vehicle high voltage parts.

This work must only be done by qualified EV mechanics and technicians wearing special personal protective equipment (PPE).

Gloves (PPE)

High-voltage PPE gloves are designed to protect the hands from electric shock when working with high-voltage systems.

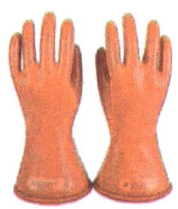

Eye protection (PPE)

Eye protection is available in various formats. It is primarily designed to provide protection against impact, heat, chemicals, and fumes.

Workwear (PPE)

Specific workwear or overalls provide an additional layer of protection between the user and potential hazards

Footwear (PPE)

High-voltage overshoes are a type of protective footwear designed to protect feet from electric shock when working with high-voltage systems.

Electric Vehicles Explained

Chapter 6.
Maintenance Made Simple

Cells are small individual units inside a battery that store energy and combine together to provide the power needed for the battery to work.

Nickel metal hydride (Ni-MH) is a type of rechargeable battery that stores energy and is commonly used in older hybrid cars. The name comes from the metals and chemicals inside.

Lithium-ion (Li-ion) batteries are rechargeable batteries that store a lot of energy in a small, lightweight package, commonly used in modern electric cars and many other devices. The name comes from the metals and chemicals inside.

Motor/Generator

Powerful motors, usually hidden within the car's transmission system, make the car move. When these motors get electricity, they start turning. When the motor is turned, it also makes some electricity that can help charge the car's main battery. Because these motors both drive the car and help generate electricity, they are called motor-generators.

High voltage cables

High-voltage energy in electric vehicles is kept separate from the rest of the car through fully insulated cables. These cables are usually bright orange to show they are high voltage. However, the colour is not standardised on some micro and mild hybrids, so you should be careful around any brightly coloured wires in a hybrid or electric vehicle.

Electric Vehicles Explained

Chapter 6.
Maintenance Made Simple

The cables usually have an inner core made from copper or aluminium strands, coated in protective insulation, often plastic or rubber, to stop the electrical voltage from leaking to other parts of the car.

 Whenever you see orange cables or connectors in an electric vehicle, always assume they are live and could be dangerous.

Be cautious and never touch them.

Inverter converters

Electric vehicle drive batteries store and use direct current (DC). Most vehicle drive motors use alternating current (AC). To allow these parts to work together, a special component called an inverter/converter is used to change DC to AC and back again. You'll typically find it in a metal box near the electrical drive system, either at the front or rear of the vehicle. While its size can vary depending on the vehicle, it usually has large orange cables connecting it to the battery and drive motors.

Electric Vehicles Explained

Chapter 6.
Maintenance Made Simple

DC to DC converters

Electric cars also have a small 12-volt battery, similar to the ones in traditional cars. This is used to initially switch the car on and powers important things like security, lights, wipers, and entertainment systems when the car is off. However, once you turn the car on, the main battery takes over and supplies power to the whole car through a special device called a DC-to-DC converter that steps-down high voltage to low voltage. It also keeps the 12-volt battery charged; this way, the smaller battery doesn't get drained quickly.

Normally, the 12-volt battery in an electric car doesn't have to do much once the car is running, which means it can be smaller and lighter. But if you use it too much without turning the car on, it can run out of power, just like in a regular car. This is why it's essential to know how to jump-start your electric vehicle if needed and follow the manufacturer instructions carefully.

JUMP STARTING

Electric vehicles (EVs) can often be jump started similarly to traditional cars. It's important to follow the manufacturer's instructions and precautions, which are usually found in the vehicle handbook.

Electric Vehicles Explained

Chapter 6.
Maintenance Made Simple

There are a few types of jump-starting power sources available:

- Another vehicle or a charged 12-volt battery using jump leads.
- A jump pack, which is a dedicated tool with its own internal battery and clamps to connect to the non-starting vehicle.
- A boost pack, which is smaller than a jump pack, and uses a capacitor to store and release the electrical energy needed for jump starting.

Some boost packs might not work with the jump start points because they need to connect directly to the 12-volt auxiliary battery. Many jump start points are linked to the low voltage system through the DC-to-DC converter and might not let the boost pack function properly. It's important not to press any override button on the boost pack, as the high energy might cause serious damage.

Always follow the manufacturer's instructions.

Electric Vehicles Explained

Chapter 6.
Maintenance Made Simple

Many 12-volt batteries in EVs are hidden behind panels, so access might be limited. If this is the case, manufacturers often provide specific jump start points near the fuse box area. You can check the location in the vehicle handbook.

Usually, only a positive connection is provided, and the negative should be connected to a suitable ground point nearby.

Positive (+) and negative (-) refer to the two ends of a battery or electrical circuit. The positive end gives out electrical energy, and the negative end takes in electrical energy.

A ground point is a place, normally on a vehicle chassis or frame, where you connect a cable to complete an electrical circuit safely.

Never connect the positive to the negative or vice versa, as this might cause severe damage.

Follow the instructions on the jump starter, connect the positive first and the negative second. Once the connections are made, switch the EV to ready mode, and then disconnect the jump leads in the reverse order.

OBC units

Charging an electric vehicle from a mains supply creates a challenge because the car's high voltage battery needs direct current (DC), but the mains supply provides alternating current (AC). So, every electric car needs a converter to change

AC to DC to charge the battery from any normal power source. This converter is called the onboard charger or OBC.

Electric Vehicles Explained

Chapter 6.
Maintenance Made Simple

The onboard charger (OBC) in an electric vehicle (EV) has three main jobs.

- First, it turns the power from mains electricity into the right kind of power to charge the car's battery. (AC to DC)
- Second, it communicates with the charging equipment to ensure everything works smoothly.
- Lastly, it controls the charging process to keep everything safe, efficient, and help the battery last longer.

Because the onboard charger needs to change AC power from the mains to the DC power that the car's battery uses, this part often slows down the charging. The process of converting between these two types of power takes time. Also, the quality and design of the onboard charger can affect how fast it works. This means that two similar cars might charge at different speeds depending on the onboard chargers they have, even if the power supply is the same.

The only exception is when using DC rapid charging equipment. With DC rapid charging, the power is changed from AC to DC before it gets to the car. This means that if your vehicle can use rapid charging, the onboard charger can be bypassed, making the process much faster. However, to keep things safe and prolong the battery's life, rapid charging usually stops at 80% capacity.

Electric Vehicles Explained

Chapter 6.
Maintenance Made Simple

AIR CONDITIONING

Air conditioning, sometimes called HVAC (Heating, Ventilation and Air Conditioning), is important not only for keeping you comfortable, but it also helps your electric vehicle work better.

Air conditioning works a lot like a refrigerator, moving special chemicals around a closed system. As these chemicals travel, they change between liquid and gas at different points, which either absorbs heat (cooling things down) or releases heat (warming things up).

With one radiator inside the car (called an evaporator) and one outside (called a condenser), heat can be moved from inside the car to the outside air, keeping the cabin cool. This process also removes moisture and dirt from the air, making it cleaner and more pleasant to breathe.

 Dehumidifying the cabin air makes the passenger compartment more comfortable for the occupants. If air conditioning is combined with the heater, it can also help quickly clear foggy windows on damp days.

Dehumidifying means removing extra moisture from the air to make it less humid and more comfortable to breath.

Electric Vehicles Explained

Chapter 6.
Maintenance Made Simple

The air conditioning system in electric vehicles can also help keep the high voltage drive batteries at the right temperature. It does this either by having a separate cooling part for the batteries or by using the same air that cools the cabin. By ensuring the air conditioning works correctly, you can help your electric vehicle's battery run more efficiently and safely.

To move and control the special chemicals in an air conditioning system, cars with engines use a pump called a **compressor**. This pump was powered by a belt connected to the engine. Since electric vehicles don't have engines, they use an electric pump powered by the car's high voltage battery to run their air conditioning.

Regularly servicing and maintaining the air conditioning system is important because it ensures everything runs smoothly and keeps you comfortable. It also helps the car's battery operate safely and last longer. Only qualified technicians should do this maintenance because the chemicals used can be harmful to the environment, and there are rules about how they should be handled. Also, since an electric pump is used, a special oil that doesn't conduct electricity is needed to lubricate the compressor. Using the wrong oil could cause an electrical leak, which can be very dangerous.

 A **compressor** is a pump that moves special chemicals in an air conditioning system to create cold air inside your car.

Electric Vehicles Explained

Chapter 6.
Maintenance Made Simple

 When using heating, ventilation and air conditioning HVAC, directing warm air to the footwells can help the cabin heat up quicker as hot air rises. Directing cold air upwards will have the opposite effect, cooling the cabin down quicker.

PTC heaters

The cabin of an electric car needs heating to keep its passengers comfortable in winter. Traditional cars use heated engine coolant that flows through a radiator inside the car, with an electric fan to blow the warm air through vents. In hybrid and fully electric cars, there might not be engine coolant for this job. Instead, a PTC heater is used.

PTC, or **positive temperature coefficient**, is just a fancy way of saying it uses electrical resistance to create heat. Basically, a PTC heater is an electric heater by another name.

When electricity flows through the heater, it warms up due to **resistance**. This warmth can then be used to heat the inside of the car. A PTC heater works like a kettle or toaster, warming up a liquid or air, which is then used to heat the car quickly. Unlike traditional cars that need engine heat, EVs can start heating as soon as they are turned on. You can even set them to preheat before your trip, ensuring a cosy ride from the moment you get in.

Electric Vehicles Explained

Chapter 6.
Maintenance Made Simple

A **positive temperature coefficient (PTC)** means that as the temperature of a material increases, its electrical resistance also increases.

Resistance is a measure of how much a material slows down the flow of electricity through it.

If preheating is conducted while mains charging, the electrical energy comes from the supply and not from the vehicle battery, maintaining driving range.

When you use the cabin heater in electric cars and hybrids, it runs on the main battery, which can drain the battery and reduce how far you can drive.

To help with this, some car makers offer other options like heated seats and steering wheels.

These use power from a smaller battery system, so they don't take as much energy from the main battery but still keep you warm and comfy.

Chapter 6.
Maintenance Made Simple

MAINTENANCE AND REPAIRS

BATTERY CARE

One of the most critical aspects of EV maintenance is battery care. Electric car owners should regularly monitor the battery's state of charge (SoC) and avoid letting it drop too low. Most manufacturers recommend maintaining a charge level between 20% and 80% for everyday use to extend battery lifespan.

Additionally, periodic checks for software updates are essential, as these can improve battery management systems and overall vehicle performance.

In a similar way to computer, or mobile phone updates, many manufacturers provide over-the-air updates, making it easier for owners to keep their vehicles up to date without the need for a service visit.

Electric Vehicles Explained

Chapter 6.
Maintenance Made Simple

Despite common concerns, EV batteries are not like phone batteries and last much longer.

Many car manufacturers offer extensive warranties, such as eight years or 100,000miles. Studies and real-world data show that EV batteries rarely need replacement and maintain a high capacity even after many miles.

In fact, experts believe EV batteries often outlast the cars themselves, making them a reliable option for long-term use.

TYRE MAINTENANCE

Tyre maintenance is another important consideration for electric vehicle owners. EVs tend to be heavier due to their battery packs, which can lead to increased tyre wear. Regularly checking tyre pressure and tread depth is crucial for safety and efficiency. Properly inflated tyres not only enhance driving range but also improve handling and reduce wear.

Electric Vehicles Explained

Chapter 6.
Maintenance Made Simple

🚗 HOW TO CHECK AND INFLATE TYRES

Before you start, gather these tools:

A tyre pressure gauge - This can be digital or manual and helps you measure tyre pressure accurately.

An air compressor - You can use a portable one or the one available at a fuel station to inflate the tyres.

Owner's manual - This will tell you the recommended tyre pressure for your specific EV model.

🚗 CHECKING TYRE PRESSURE

Follow these steps to check your tyre pressure:

Step 1
- Find the Recommended Pressure
- Consult your owner's manual or the sticker sometimes located on the driver's side door pillar. This will indicate the manufacturer's recommended tyre pressure, usually measured in pounds per square inch (PSI), kilopascals (kPa) or as barometric (Bar) value. Make sure you use the correct unit on the gauge.

Step 2
- Prepare Your Tyres
- It's best to check tyre pressure when the tyres are cold, as heat can cause them to expand and give inaccurate readings. Ensure your vehicle has been parked forat least three hours or driven less than a mile.

Electric Vehicles Explained

Chapter 6.
Maintenance Made Simple

Step 3
- Remove the Valve Cap
- Locate the valve stem on each tyre and remove the cap. Keep the caps in a safe place to avoid losing them.

Step 4
- Attach the Pressure Gauge
- Place the tyre pressure gauge onto the valve stem and press down firmly. You should hear a brief hiss as air escapes which then stops, indicating that the gauge is correctly attached. The gauge will then display the current pressure.

Step 5
- Read the Pressure
- Note the reading on the gauge. Compare it with the recommended pressure from your owner's manual. Repeat this process for all four tyres.

INFLATING TYRES

If any tyre pressure is below the recommended level, follow these steps to inflate them:

Step 1
- Use an Air Compressor
- Many fuel stations have air compressors, but you can also use a portable compressor if you have one. Attach the compressor's hose to the valve stem, ensuring a secure fit.

Electric Vehicles Explained

Chapter 6.
Maintenance Made Simple

Step 2
- Inflate the Tyre
- Activate the compressor and begin inflating the tyre. Monitor the pressure with your gauge to avoid over-inflation. Add air in short bursts, checking the pressure frequently.

Step 3
- Check the Pressure Again
- If a separate pressure gauge has been used, after inflating, remove the compressor hose and immediately check the tyre pressure with your gauge. If the pressure is still too low, repeat the process. If it's too high, release some air by pressing the gauge's bleed button or gently pressing the valve stem.

Step 3
- Replace the Valve Cap
- Once the tyre is inflated to the correct pressure, replace the valve cap securely. Repeat this process for any other tyres that need inflating.

Check Monthly: Make it a habit to check your tyre pressure at least once a month.

Before Long Trips: Always check tyre pressure before going on long journeys.

Weather Considerations: Tyre pressure can change with temperature, so check more often during extreme weather.

Electric Vehicles Explained

Chapter 6.
Maintenance Made Simple

Why tyre pressure matters

Tyres are the only part of your EV that touches the road. So, keeping them in good shape and at the right pressure is crucial.

Proper tyre pressure ensures:

Safety - The right pressure helps tyres grip the road properly, reducing the chance of accidents.

Efficiency - Well-inflated tyres make your EV more efficient, helping it go further on a single charge.

Longevity - Maintaining good pressure prevents uneven wear, meaning your tyres last longer.

Punctures

Many electric cars no longer have a spare wheel for emergencies. This is often because of limited storage space, weight-saving reasons, or simply to cut costs. Instead, many cars come with a canister of tyre sealant and a simple way to inflate the tyre if you get a puncture. If the puncture isn't too bad, you can use the sealant through the tyre's inflation valve to get the car to a safe place.

Remember, tyre sealant is just a temporary fix and should only be used in an emergency. Don't drive on a damaged tyre for too long.

Electric Vehicles Explained

Chapter 6.
Maintenance Made Simple

Tyre sealant will degrade over time, meaning it should be replaced regularly.

Check the expiry date of any sealant supplied with the car and make a note of it, so you know when to buy new sealant.

Jacking Points

Because an EV's high-voltage battery is usually under the car floor, it's really important to follow the manufacturer's instructions when lifting the car with a jack.

Placing the jack in the wrong spot can damage the battery or twist the car's frame, which might void your warranty or safety features, and could even cause a short circuit leading to a fire.

Manufacturers not only tell you where to place the jack, but some also require special lifting pads or blocks made for your specific car. Always use these to keep safe and protect your EV.

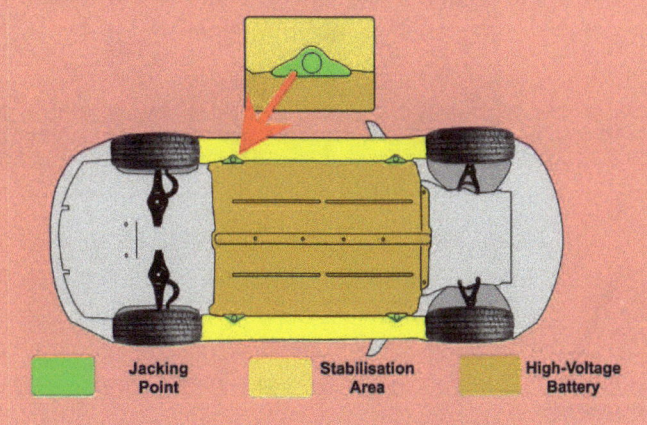

Electric Vehicles Explained

Chapter 6.
Maintenance Made Simple

 **BRAKES**

Brakes in electric cars need attention, but they work a bit differently from traditional cars. Many EVs use regenerative braking, which helps slow the car down and turns that energy back into electricity for the battery. This means brake pads can last longer than in regular cars. However, it's still important to check the brakes regularly to make sure everything is working well. If you hear any strange noises or notice anything unusual when braking, it's a sign to get it looked at by a professional.

 It's important to have your brakes checked by professionals who know what they're doing.

This is crucial to make sure your car stays safe and works properly.

Electric Vehicles Explained

Chapter 6.
Maintenance Made Simple

❄ AIR CONDITIONING

Air conditioning in your EV needs regular check-ups and maintenance. It's important to have it serviced and re-gassed from time to time. The air

conditioning system works best when it has the right amount of refrigerant chemicals, which are essential for keeping the car cool and comfortable.

These chemicals can slowly decrease over time, so it's a good idea to get the system checked every year. This not only keeps you comfortable but also helps control the temperature of the EV's battery, which can be important for some electric cars.

Regular air conditioning checks should be done by qualified professionals.

It's important because the air conditioning system keeps you comfortable and helps manage the temperature of the car's battery.

Only professionals are allowed to maintain it because of safety and environmental laws.

Electric Vehicles Explained

Chapter 6.
Maintenance Made Simple

🚗 WATER AND WASHING

It's important that electric car parts are kept as waterproof as possible. However, remember that everything ages over time, and this includes waterproofing. Seals or gaskets can wear out and fail with age or road damage, which could let water in during extreme situations. Washing an electric car by hand or using a car wash usually isn't a problem but be careful when using a pressure washer around sensitive high-voltage parts to make sure water doesn't get past seals or gaskets.

It is also important to know that many electric cars have their batteries located under the floor. This means they shouldn't be driven through deep water like floods or rivers. Each electric car has a maximum wading depth, which can be found in the vehicle's manual. It's a good idea to check this information as soon as you get your car to avoid any issues.

Chapter 6.
Maintenance Made Simple

While electric vehicles are designed to be safe, it's important to remember that water can still cause damage to the car's electrical systems, especially if it gets into high-voltage parts. This can lead to long-term issues and failures.

The safety systems in place help to reduce the risk of injury, but they shouldn't be relied on completely.

It's always best to be cautious and avoid driving through deep water to protect your EV.

 SOFTWARE UPDATES

Over-the-air (OTA) updates are a modern technological advancement that allows electric vehicles to receive software updates wirelessly, just like how smartphones get their updates.

OTA updates allow your electric car to receive new software and improvements without needing any cables or visits to the service centre. Just like your smartphone, your car can get these updates over the internet, making it simple and convenient to keep everything up-to-date.

When a carmaker releases a new update for their electric vehicles, they send it to the cars over the internet.

Electric Vehicles Explained

Chapter 6.
Maintenance Made Simple

First, you get a notification on your car's display screen or app that a new update is available. Next, the car downloads the update using its internet connection, either through cellular data or Wi-Fi. Then, the update is installed in your car's system. To do this safely, your car needs to be parked and not in use. Finally, much like rebooting a smartphone, your car might need to restart its system to finish the update.

These updates are an easy and convenient way to keep your EV running smoothly with the latest features and improvements.

Why Are OTA updates important

OTA updates bring many benefits to both the car manufacturer and the car owner:

Convenience - Owners do not need to visit a dealership or service centre to get the latest software updates, saving time and effort.

Enhanced features - Manufacturers can add new features and functionalities to vehicles even after they have been purchased. For example, a new navigation system feature or an improvement in the car's performance.

Bug fixes and security - OTA updates can fix software bugs, patch security holes, and make overall system stability better, ensuring a safer and more reliable driving experience.

Performance improvements - Updates can optimise the car's software, resulting in better battery management, more efficient driving modes, and a better user experience.

Chapter 6.
Maintenance Made Simple

To make sure your electric vehicle gets and installs these over-the-air (OTA) updates successfully, follow these simple steps:

Keep your car connected to the internet, either through a good mobile signal or a reliable Wi-Fi connection. Watch out for update notifications and follow any instructions given by the car manufacturer. Plan to install updates when your car isn't being used, like overnight or when it will be parked for a long time. Make sure your car's battery is charged enough to avoid any interruptions during the update process.

Over-the-air updates are a fantastic and easy way to keep your electric vehicle in top shape. By knowing how these updates work and making sure your car is set up to get them, you can enjoy a better driving experience with the latest features and improvements delivered straight to your car.

CONCLUSION

Maintaining your electric vehicle is crucial for ensuring its longevity and optimal performance. Regular maintenance not only extends the life of your vehicle but also maximises its efficiency and reliability, ultimately contributing to a more sustainable and enjoyable journey on the road.

Chapter 7. Building Confidence as an EV Driver

Building confidence as a new electric vehicle (EV) owner starts with understanding and becoming comfortable with your car.

Here are some simple steps to get you started on your journey:

Practice driving - Spend time getting to know your EV by driving it regularly. Familiarise yourself with the car's controls, acceleration, and braking, which might feel different from traditional cars due to the instant **torque** of electric motors.

Chapter 7. Building Confidence as an EV Driver

Learn charging - Practice charging your EV at home and at public charging stations. This will help you feel more confident when plugging in your car. Know the locations of nearby charging stations and how to use them. Explore payment options for public charging stations and download any required apps.

Seek support - Join EV communities, both online and locally. These groups offer a wealth of tips, experiences, and support from fellow EV owners. They can provide valuable insights into making the most out of your electric car.

Understand your EV - Take the time to read the manual and understand the specific features and capabilities of your electric car. Knowing your vehicle's **range**, charging time, and unique features will make you feel more in control.

Consider safety - Aspects of your EV, such as charging safety, battery maintenance, and pedestrian safety awareness are very important. Proper charging practices are crucial to avoid electrical issues and ensure your EV operates efficiently. Regular maintenance of the battery and other systems ensures longevity and prevents unexpected failures. Additionally, be mindful of pedestrians, as EVs are quieter and might not be easily noticed by those around you.

Celebrate progress - Every eco-friendly mile you drive is a step towards a more sustainable future. Acknowledge small victories and improvements in your driving and charging habits.

By following these steps and embracing the learning process, you'll soon find yourself a confident and knowledgeable EV owner, ready to enjoy all the benefits that come with driving electric.

Chapter 7. Building Confidence as an EV Driver

Torque is the force that makes something rotate or turn. In electric cars, it means how strongly the motor can make the wheels spin.

Range refers to the distance an electric vehicle can travel on a single charge before it needs to be recharged. It tells you how far you can drive your car without stopping to recharge the battery.

CONVENIENCE

One of the most convenient aspects of owning an electric vehicle is the elimination of trips to the fuel station, especially during late hours or in inclement weather. With an EV, you can charge your car at home, typically overnight, using a standard electrical outlet or a dedicated home charging station. This means waking up each morning to a fully charged car, ready for the day ahead. No more rushing to the fuel station before an early morning meeting or worrying about finding a station late at night.

Additionally, charging your EV at home is a cleaner and more pleasant experience. Gone are the days of handling pumps and dealing with the lingering smell of fuel. Instead, you simply plug in your car, much like you would charge your phone, and let it charge while you go about your daily activities. This not only saves time but also reduces exposure to harmful fumes and minimises environmental impact.

Electric Vehicles Explained

Chapter 7. Building Confidence as an EV Driver

SAFETY FEATURES

Electric vehicles are not only environmentally friendly but also packed with advanced safety features to ensure a secure driving experience. One of the standout aspects of EVs is their advanced driver-assist systems (ADAS). These systems include a range of technologies designed to help you drive more safely and confidently.

For example, many EVs come equipped with adaptive cruise control, which adjusts your car's speed to maintain a safe distance from the vehicle in front of you. This means less stress and more comfort on long drives or in heavy traffic.

Lane-keeping assist is another common feature, gently steering your car to keep it centred in its lane and alerting you if you start to drift.

Automatic emergency braking can detect potential collisions and apply the brakes if you don't react in time, significantly reducing the risk of accidents.

Blind-spot monitoring warns you of vehicles in your blind spots, making lane changes safer.

Parking sensors and cameras provide a clear view of your surroundings, helping you park with ease and avoid obstacles.

With these advanced driver-assist systems, electric vehicles offer a higher level of safety, making them an excellent choice for both new and experienced drivers.

Electric Vehicles Explained

Chapter 7. Building Confidence as an EV Driver

TECH-SAVVY OPTIONS

Electric vehicles come equipped with a range of tech-savvy options that make driving more intuitive and enjoyable. These features include touchscreens, voice commands, and smartphone integrations, which are designed to simplify and enhance your driving experience.

Touchscreens in EVs function much like the screens on your smartphone or tablet. They provide a user-friendly interface for controlling various aspects of your car, such as navigation, music, climate control, and more. With just a tap or swipe, you can easily access information and adjust settings to your preference.

 Where possible, touchscreen options should not be updated while driving as this might mean taking your eyes off the road. Do not undertake any activity which distracts your attention away from the activity of driving.

Voice commands

Voice commands add another layer of convenience by allowing you to control your car using simple spoken instructions. Instead of taking your hands off the wheel or your eyes off the road, you can say commands like "navigate to the nearest charging station" or "play my favourite playlist," and the car will respond accordingly. This hands-free functionality enhances safety and comfort while driving.

Electric Vehicles Explained

Chapter 7. Building Confidence as an EV Driver

Smartphone integration

Smartphone integrations, such as Apple CarPlay and Android Auto, seamlessly connect your phone to your car's infotainment system. This integration allows you to access your phone's apps, messages, maps, and music directly through the car's touchscreen or via voice commands. It creates a cohesive driving experience where you can stay connected and entertained without distraction.

Overall, these tech-savvy options make driving an electric vehicle a more intuitive and enjoyable experience, offering convenience, safety, and connectivity at your fingertips.

EV MUST-HAVES

When you start driving an electric vehicle, there are a few essential items that can make your experience even better. These EV must-haves will help you stay organised, prepared, and connected as you embrace this new way of driving.

First on the list is a Charging Cable Organiser. Just like keeping your headphones neatly wrapped, this organiser helps you keep your car neat, and your charging cables untangled. It ensures that you always know where your cables are and keeps them from getting damaged or dirty.

Electric Vehicles Explained

Chapter 7. Building Confidence as an EV Driver

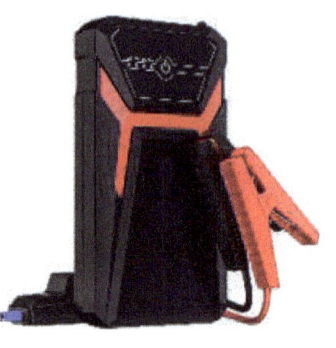

Next, consider having a Portable Power Bank. This is especially useful for emergencies on long trips, to keep your electronic accessories such as mobile phones or tablets charged and ready for use.

Some portable Power Banks can act as a 12 volt jump starter in the event of a discharged auxiliary battery. It's a handy backup that gives you peace of mind.

Since many EVs no longer come with a spare wheel, a tyre pump is particularly useful if you get a flat tyre.

Today's small electric tyre inflators are convenient and simple to use. They either plug into your car's power socket or run on a rechargeable battery. These inflators are compact and can be easily stored in your car, offering a handy solution in case of an emergency.

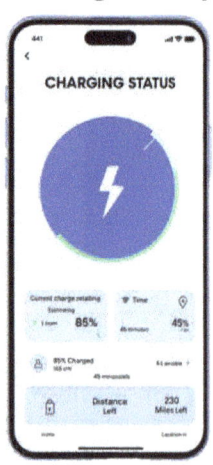

Another essential is EV Apps.

These smartphone applications allow you to manage charging, track your vehicle's range, and find charging stations easily.

They are like your digital co-pilot, helping you plan your trips and make the most of your EV's capabilities.

Electric Vehicles Explained

Chapter 7. Building Confidence as an EV Driver

FINALLY

Embracing the EV lifestyle is an exciting and fulfilling journey, especially for those venturing into the world of electric vehicles for the first time. Here are some simple steps to help you get started and make the most out of your EV experience:

Celebrate savings

One of the biggest advantages of driving an electric vehicle is the savings on fuel and maintenance. Keep track of how much you save each month by switching from conventional fuel to electricity. This not only helps you appreciate the economic benefits but also reinforces your decision to go green.

Electric Vehicles Explained

Chapter 7. Building Confidence as an EV Driver

Spread awareness

Sharing your EV journey with friends and family can inspire others to consider making the switch. Talk about the positive aspects of owning an electric vehicle, such as reduced emissions, the convenience of charging at home, and the enjoyable driving experience. Your enthusiasm can be contagious and encourage more people to adopt sustainable practices.

Enjoy the ride

Driving an EV offers a unique experience with its quiet operation, smooth acceleration, and eco-friendly nature. Take the time to appreciate these features and enjoy the tranquillity and comfort they provide. Whether you're commuting to work or taking a road trip, the pleasant driving experience of an EV is something to relish.

By following these steps, you'll not only embrace the EV lifestyle but also contribute to a greener and more sustainable future. So, get ready to embark on this rewarding journey and enjoy the many benefits that come with driving electric.

Owning an EV is a rewarding, empowering step toward modern, sustainable living. With these simple tips, you'll be navigating the electric car lifestyle with ease and confidence.

Enjoy the journey.

Electric Vehicles Explained